today's city houses

Edition 2005

Author: Pilar Chueca
Publisher: Arian Mostaedi
Editorial Coordinator: Jacobo Krauel
Graphic designer & production: Pilar Chueca, Marta Rojals
Text: contributed by the architects, edited by Núria Rodríguez

© Carles Broto i Comerma
Jonqueres, 10, 1-5
08003 Barcelona, Spain
Tel.: +34 93 301 21 99
 Fax: +34-93-301 00 21
E-mail: info@linksbooks.net
www. linksbooks.net

today's city houses

structure

INTRODUCTION

In the complicated exercise of lilling the voids in the metropolitan puzzle and bringing the pieces together, fitting a volume into the city's narrow, cramped niches is a delicate and difficult task for architects.

Aesthetic and functional considerations alike come into play in this complex chore. On the one hand, closure between two existing volumes is sought, linking the existing elements into a single unit that merges the new building with the two that flank it; while on the other, a subtle, distinct language must be developed for a particularly squeezed in facade.

As the barrier between the street and the private interior, the most interesting compositional and structutal aspects of the project are brought together on the facade. It is the face of the building, a privileged, outward looking vantage point, which embraces the neighboring buildings to form the urban fabric and linj up with the artery of the city into which it is woven. Behind this curtain of stone, glass or concrete we find a narrow and constrained space which challenges the architect's mastery in performing the seemingly impossible task of creating a layout with all the necessary facilities, while also giving it a feel of spaciousness and balance.

Based on recent examples by internationally renowned architects, this detailed study analyzes the difficulty of fitting new residential volumes, with exemplary technical and formal solutions, into tight, difficult sites, while also embracing the surrounding context. Included is a wide sampling of projects in which the architects perform juggling acts in astutely economizing on space in order to put into effect a judicious forulation of functional and aesthetic requirements.

Kohki Hiranuma /
Hs Workshop - ASIA

MINNA no IE

Kusatsu-shi Shiga, Japan

This three-story house has a total floor area of just under 100m^2 and was designed for two households together comprising six people. The average height of the inhabitants is relatively short, around 1.5 meters, which led to the idea of creating a project centered around the small-sized volume on a human scale.

The site is rectangular and measures 11 x 8 meters. The clients' demands, paired with local building regulations, created a "condition" for the architect, the objective of which was developed within a "representation".

The first basic condition projected a matrix of 6.4m^2. The generational gap is reflected in the shift to the left and right, upward and downward of the floors. In the process of adjusting these conditions, this gap is lessened if the floors shift 0.3 meters in direction XY.

With these requisites, an expressive method is introduced that is also reflected in the horizontal timber frame structure.

All the lines of the structure are distributed in the four directions so that an arc of 10 meters in diameter is inversely repeated along the midsection of the building. Thus, the requirements have been met, and the gaps bridged.

Photographs: Hs Workshop - ASIA

Concept diagram

Process diagram

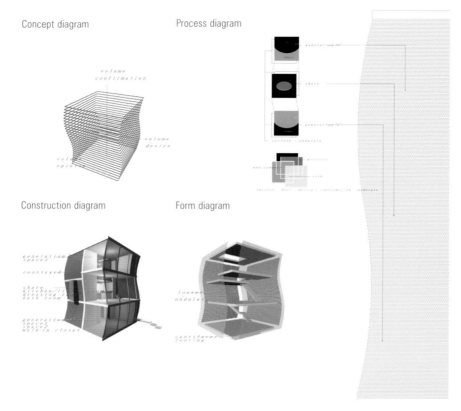

Construction diagram

Form diagram

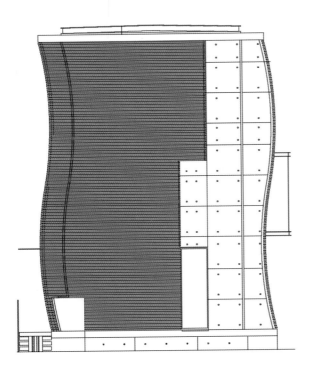

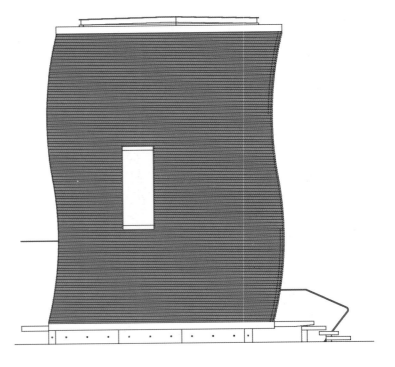

The house is a representation of the generational gap among the inhabitants destined to live in it: the exterior profile, which the architect refers to as "fluctuation-movement", is an allegory of these differences, allowing each individual to feel and speak through movement.

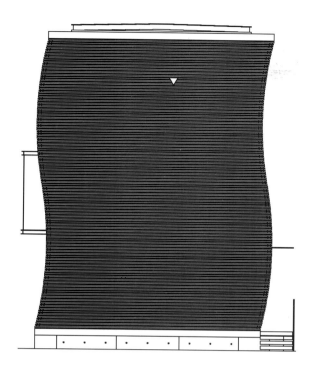
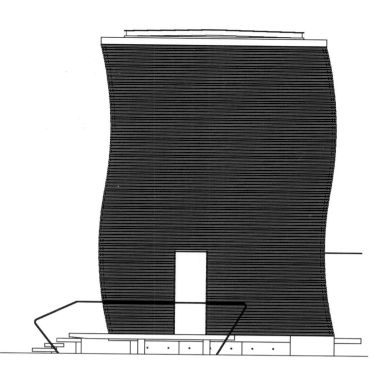

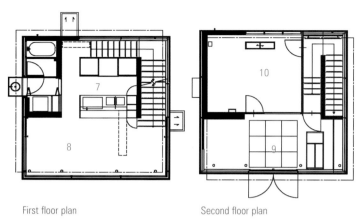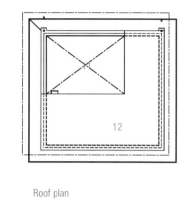

Ground floor plan

First floor plan

Second floor plan

Roof plan

1. Walkway
2. Entrance
3. Courtyard
4. Space 2
5. Space 1
6. Walk-in closet

7. Kitchen
8. Space 3
9. Space 4
10. Terrace
11. Void
12. Roof

0   1   2 m

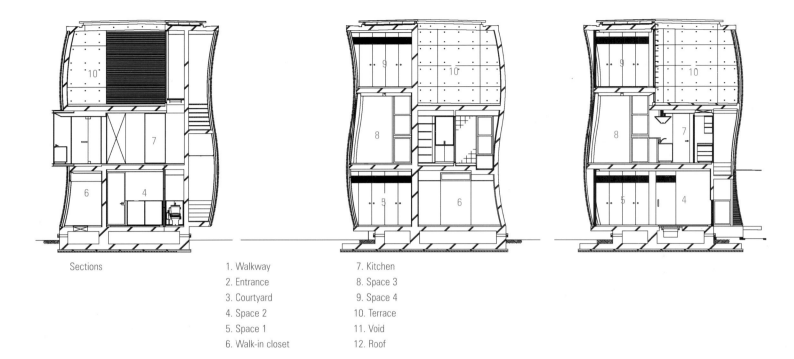

Sections

1. Walkway
2. Entrance
3. Courtyard
4. Space 2
5. Space 1
6. Walk-in closet

7. Kitchen
8. Space 3
9. Space 4
10. Terrace
11. Void
12. Roof

In the interior, each floor scarcely reaches 40m² of floor area, yet each inhabitant nonetheless enjoys personal space. This was one of the clients' requirements: a "condition" that the architect worked into a "representation" in the project.

Lorcan O´Herlihy Architects
Vertical House

Venice, California, USA

This house in Southern California responds imaginatively to the constraints of a small site, rejecting the usual front and backyard in favor of balanced articulation of the skin on all faces and in a vertical direction. Rather than sealing the sides and bringing light into the house through the front and back elevations, the architects were determined to bring in sunlight on all four sides, resulting in a simple shape with 105 vertical slit windows positioned to frame the most desirable views.

A simple material, cement board, was used in conjunction with three types of glazing. The focus is on surface manipulation, with the architecture defined through the envelope of the volume rather than the volume itself. The design is based on a steel framed cube that makes maximum use of the 25 x 55 foot footprint and frees the skin from structural restraints, allowing an unrestricted rhythm of glazing, channel glass and solid panels.

The ground floor is cut away to provide a double car port with a studio at the back. The second floor contains the master and guest bedrooms. The third floor houses the living room, kitchen and dining. There is a core volume pulled away from the perimeter that houses the main stair, cabinets and storage.

Verticality is again expressed in the central core, which extends beyond the roof for views of the Pacific Ocean three blocks away. A glass walled pavilion is located on the roof terrace which serves as an outdoor room with ocean views. Vertical House is a serene light box on a cramped infill lot which still celebrates the idea of a home.

Photographs: Michael Weschler

To maximize usable square footage, the site restrictions were pushed to the limits in both plan and height requirements, forcing the linearity of the design on paper to be translated into built form. The design avoids the "tunnel effect", creating light-filled, open interior spaces.

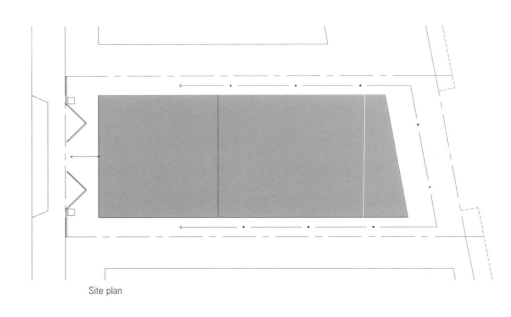

Site plan

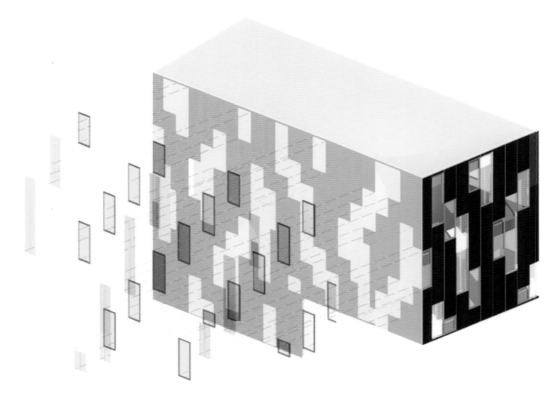

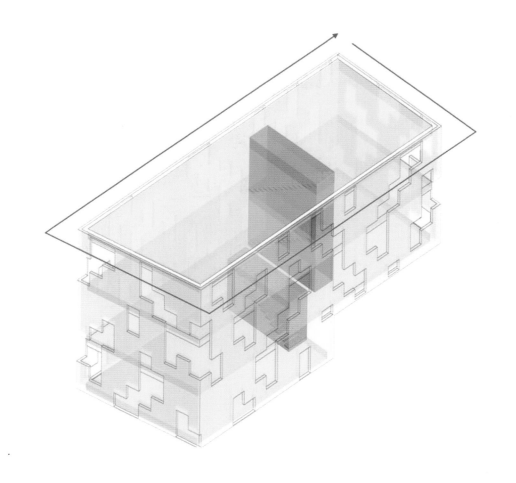

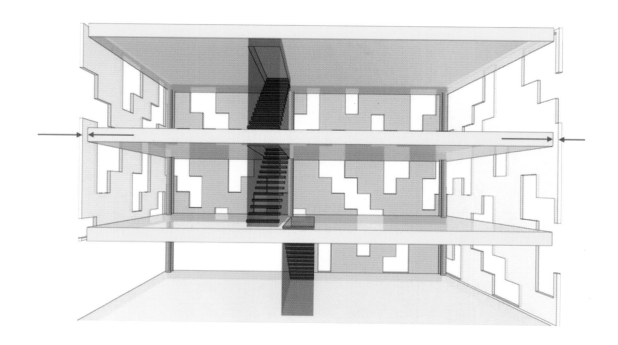

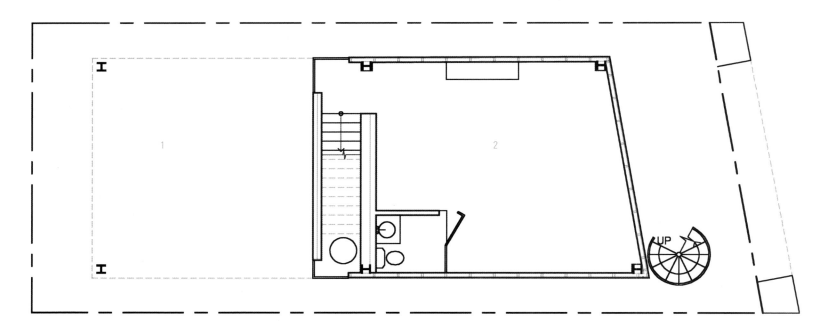

Ground floor plan
1. Double car port
2. Studio

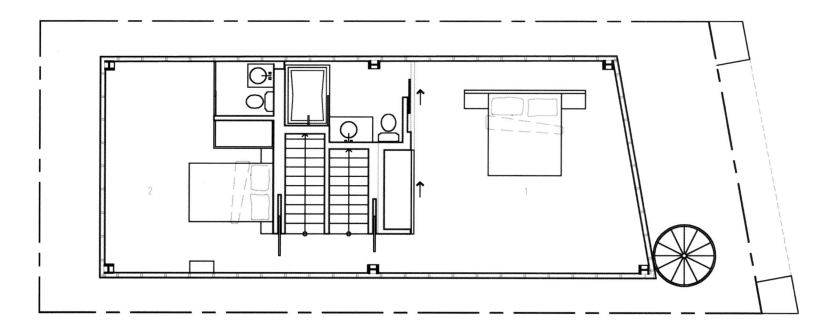

First floor plan
1. Master bedroom
2. Guest bedroom

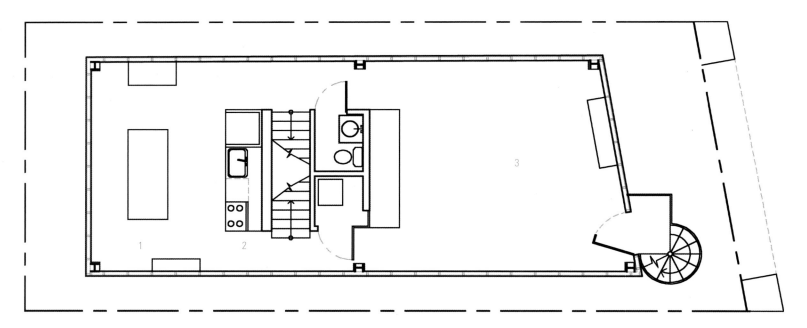

Second floor plan
1. Dining room
2. Kitchen
3. Living room

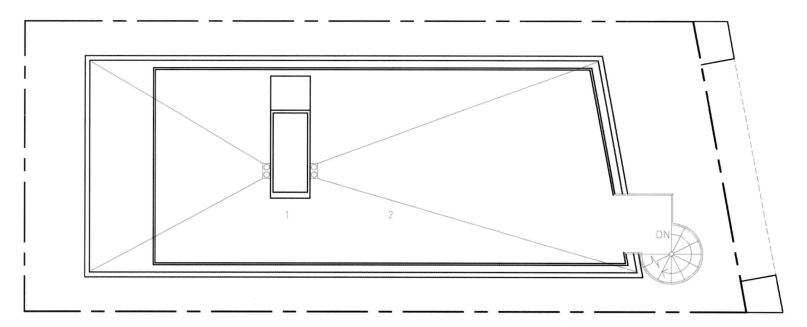

Roof plan
1. Glass Pavilion
2. Roof terrace

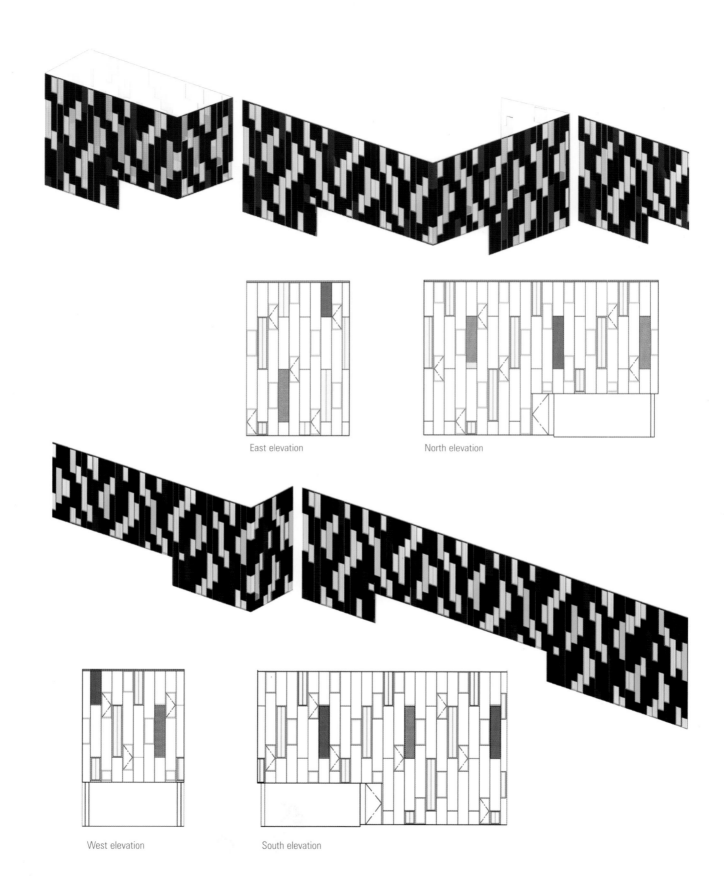

East elevation

North elevation

West elevation

South elevation

28

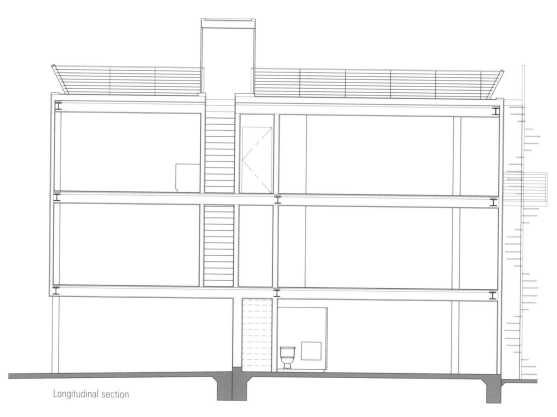

Longitudinal section

Christian Pottgiesser

House in Rue Galvani

Paris, France

The project for this house, designed to accommodate seven people, is the result of the extension of a private house located at the rear of a narrow 140 m² site. The brief specified maintaining the entire garden, while also allowing a new structure to be built on the site. This apparent paradox became the key to the project. Apart from the requirements of the client, an existing Japanese ailanthus and lime tree were protected by the Department of Parks and Gardens, making it virtually impossible to build on the perimeter of the site adjacent to the street. The architects also had to respect an early twentieth century regulation banning buildings of more than one story in the area, as well as trying not to obstruct views to the existing building.

The stone used for the facade is from the Parisian basin, the same as the stone used in the neighboring buildings. The walls, structural elements, floors and slab were built on-site using reinforced concrete. The principal walls of the house are solid stone and plywood, with a projected plaster finish. The stairs and windows, the sliding doors and the garage door are made from solid untreated iroko wood, and waxed teakwood is used for the parquet floors. Railway beams, pebbles and stone masonry are used in the garden.

Photographs: Gert von Bassewitz & Pascale Thomas

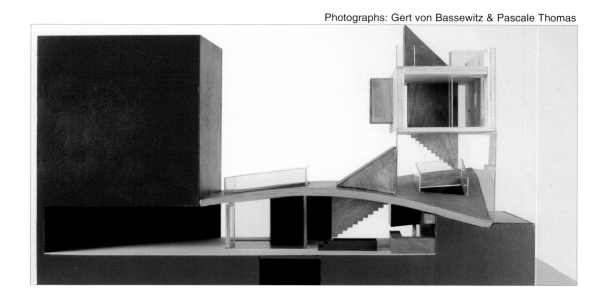

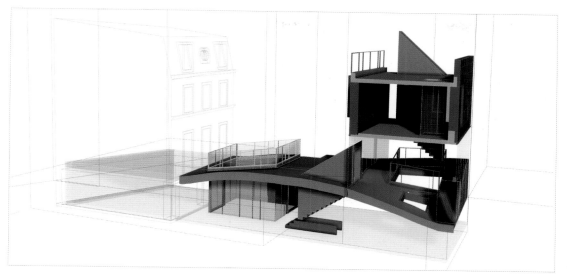

The main structuring element for the building is an irregular surface raised about 1.2 m off street level. A reinforced concrete slab rests at this level, its volume and width changing as other elements cross it or in response to circulation, lighting and layout requirements.

The brief specified that the entire garden had to be maintained, while also allowing a new structure to be built on the site. This apparent paradox became the key to the project. The actual house is located on the lower level, with the garden on the upper level. A car can be parked in the space created by the raised slab.

Longitudinal section

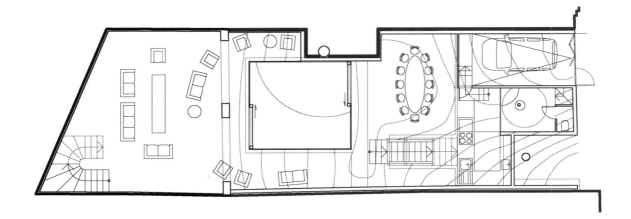

Ground floor

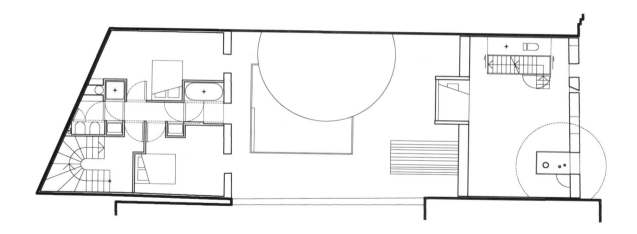

First floor

Osamu Morishita Architect and Associates

House Along the Railways

Tokyo, Japan

This house was built along busy elevated railways in Tokyo, where trains pass every three minutes and sometimes stop right outside. In order to protect it from the noise and provide privacy, a figured glass screen was built along the side facing the railway, creating a small landscaped courtyard that is the central element of the house. Instead of looking away from the train lines, big transparent windows open out to the courtyard in every room. The screen does not totally isolate the house, but it softens the noise, blurs the passing trains and directs the wind away from the house, while also providing an indoor/outdoor space with a garden oasis in the middle of the noisy metropolis.

Two families live in the house, an older couple on the first floor and their son and his family on the second floor. The two floors are connected by external stairs in the courtyard, which becomes like a big shared living room for the two separate areas.

To avoid having an unused corner in the garden, the sharp corner of the house is used as ateliers. These rooms are the least private because their transparent windows are visible from the courtyard, concentrating the gaze of the families on the ateliers.

Inside the house, all the rooms connect to each other through sliding doors in the traditional Japanese way. Private spaces can be created by closing the doors and curtains, or they can all be opened to create a large, comfortable space that makes the house feel larger than its actual size.

Photographs: Isao Imbe

40

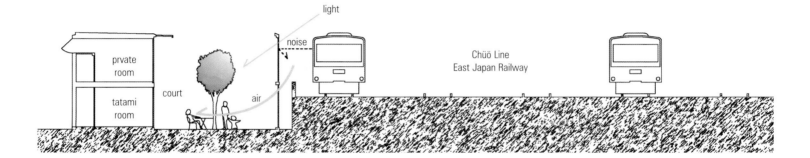

light

noise

prvate
room

tatami
room

court

air

Chüö Line
East Japan Railway

The design of this house for two families is partly conditioned by its location, adjacent to busy railway lines. The house is separated from the passing trains by a figured glass screen that softens the noise, blurs the passing trains and directs the wind away from the house. The space between this screen and the house is a landscaped courtyard shared by both families.

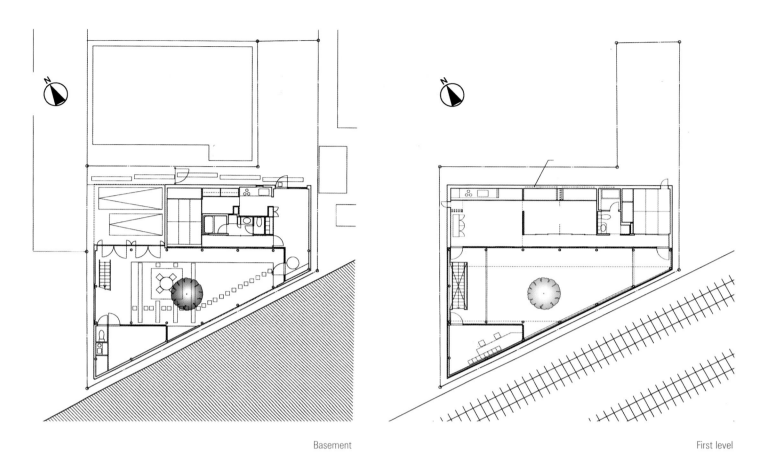

Basement   First level

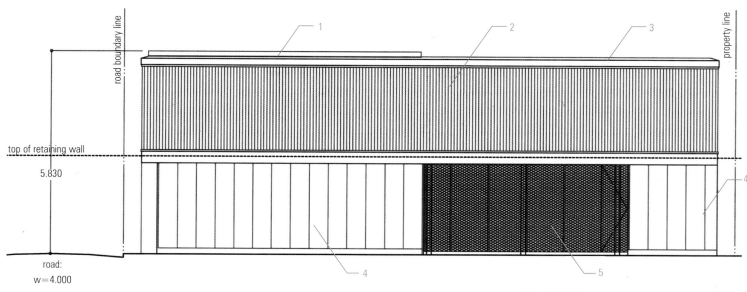

road boundary line

property line

top of retaining wall

5.830

road:
w=4.000

Façade detail

1. Parapet: stainless steel
2. Figured wired sheet glass t 6.8,
3. Top rail: galbarium steel,
   sheet metal processing
4. ACL t 100, sprayed urethane coat
5. Expanded metal, rustproof, polyurethane coat

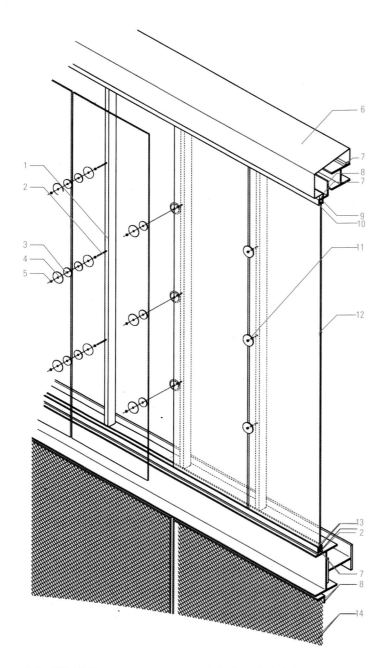

1. Steel F.B. 25x50
2. Bolt M6 stainless steel
3. Rubber sheet t 5
4. Washer o 89.1 stainless steel
5. M6 nut
6. Top rail: galbarium steel,
   sheet metal processing
7. Sealant

8. Angle steel 50x50x6
9. Steel F.B 32x6
10. Steel F.B 38x6
11. Silicone sealant
12. Figured wired sheet glass t 6.8
13. Angle steel 40x40x5
14. Expanded metal
    (one part : revolving door)

1. Top rail: galbarium steel
2. Figured wired sheet glass
3. Stainless steel
4. Steel F.B. 25x25
5. Expanded metal
6. Column
7. Figured wired sheet glass

8. Glass support
9. Aluminum sash
10. Channel steel
11. Aluminum sash
12. Exposed concrete trowel finish
13. Roof gutter: galbarium steel sheet metal processing
14. Roof: sheet waterproofing

15. Yellow cedar
16. Floor: flooring concrete slab steel deck
17. Heat insulation t25 ceiling: plasterboard
18. H-section steel 100x50x5x7
19. Tatami: RYUKYU matting floor board: panel heat insulation
20. Dampproofing sheet gravel t100

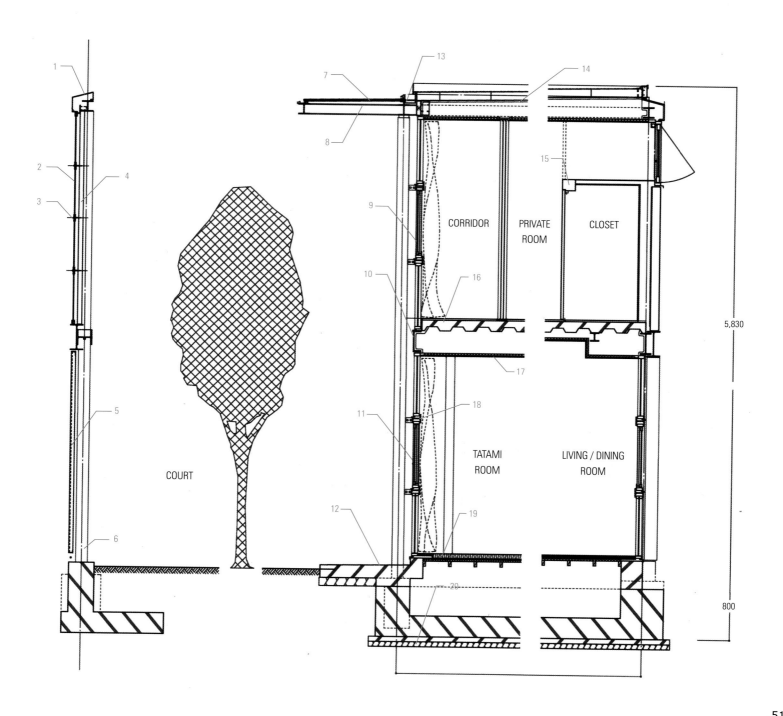

COURT

CORRIDOR

PRIVATE ROOM

CLOSET

TATAMI ROOM

LIVING / DINING ROOM

5,830

800

Benson & Forsyth

Marico House

London, UK

Located in Islington on the north bank of the Grand Union Canal, the site consisted of the shell of a derelict factory and two cottages. The single-story walls of the canal towpath and the gardens to the north, together with the two-story cottage walls which face the park and the existing houses, have been retained.

Within the house a metal valley-roof supported on perforated metal troughs and a steel frame is carried centrally on two pairs of steel columns. Externally the roof is reminiscent of a traditional Islington valley-roof, while internally it reads as a free-standing umbrella dissociated from the perimeter walls and independent of the galleries and volumes below.

The ground floor is occupied by the principal living spaces, which relate to the studio across the courtyard, or internally through the single-story dining/conference room, which may be used in conjunction with both the studio and the living floor.

The first-floor gallery contains a second living space: a dressing room and bedroom which overlook the park and the canal and extend on to the roof terrace over the single-story link into the office gallery within the studio.

The upper floor is composed of two cubes: the bathroom within a 2.1 meter cube made of opal white glass, and the main bedroom, which is located in a roof-lit enclosure suspended over the lower sitting area.

The design of the workshop section was governed by the need to maintain the two-story enclosure of the adjacent buildings on the canal side and to keep the level of the roof below the single-story wall of the gardens on the north. The roof and all of the wall planes are dissociated by glazing which washes the planes with indirect light.

Photographs: Hélène Binet

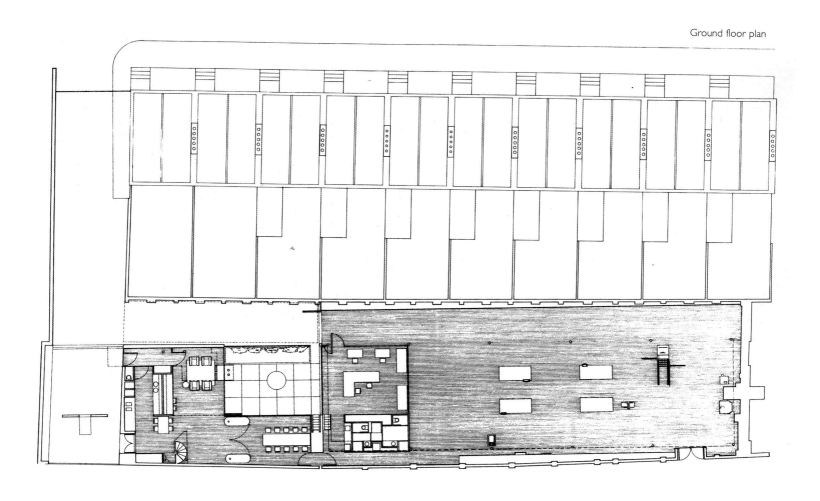

0 1 2   5 m

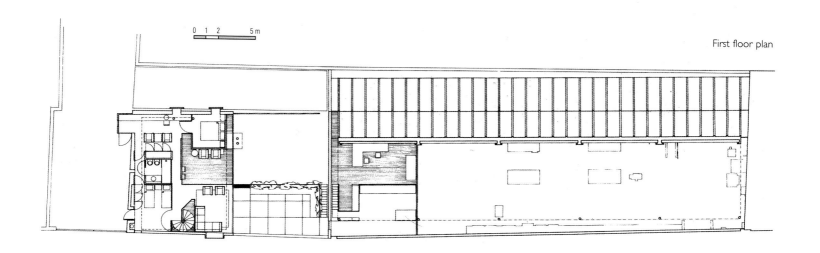

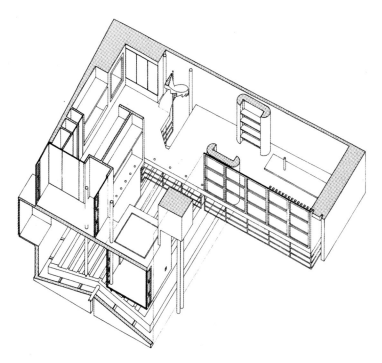

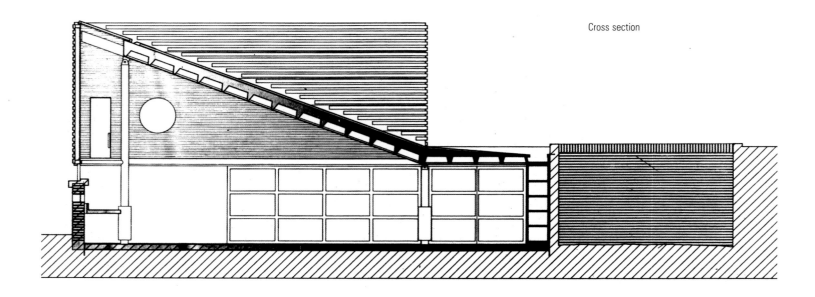

Cross section

Cross section

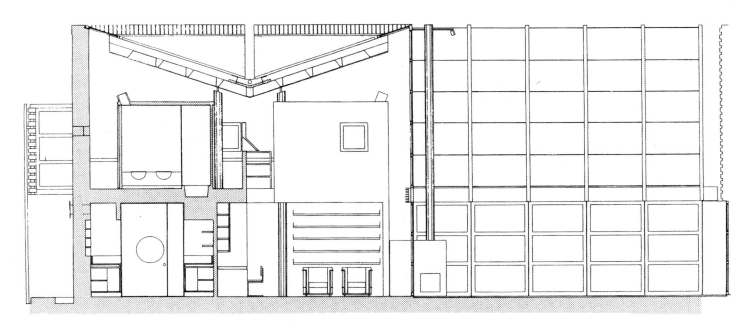

Robert M. Gurney

Fitch/O'Rourke Residence

Washington DC, USA

A thorough renovation converted this townhouse, for years the neighborhood eyesore, into a modern, warm, and intimate residence with light-filled two- and three-story spaces and a mix of rich and unexpected materials.

The owner's program included a two-bedroom, two-study residence (convertible into three bedrooms and one study) on the upper three levels, and a one-bedroom rental unit in the basement.

The project faced two serious constraints. On the one hand was the house's long, narrow footprint (63 feet long, about 17 feet wide on the front, narrowing to 13 feet), which traditionally had dictated an in-line room arrangement; and on the other was the property's location in a designated historic district, which required the front facade to be kept intact.

The renovation, which began with two brick side walls and a basement dirt floor, amounted to building a new house inside an old shell. The design for the project transcends the building's narrow confines by combining a traditional orthogonal scheme with a curving geometry (where most curves and radials trace back to a center point 28 feet east of the house) and a rotation space (based on a ten degree diagonal running from a rear corner to the center of the dining room).

The living room exploits the southern exposure and the opportunity to build a new rear facade that could bring light into a lofted space. A second lofted area near the front brings light into the northern end.

A wide range of materials was chosen to create a rich and warm mix of colors and textures and to admit and modulate light. They include concrete, steel (force-rusted, stainless, perforated, painted), block aluminum, lead-coated copper, copper wire cloth, Uniclad corrugated panels, clear and sand-blasted glass, limestone tile, maple and mahogany veneer cabinets and wall panels, and Kalwall and Lumicite translucent panels.

Photographs: Paul Warchol & Anice Hoachlander

An open well is formed by the repetition in the balcony of a 30-foot-long curved stainless steel plate adorning the kitchen floor. This simple curved opening also helps avoid the typical in-line room arrangement ordinarily dictated by such a long, narrow site.

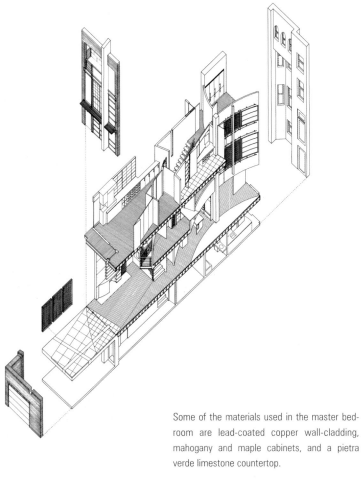

Some of the materials used in the master bedroom are lead-coated copper wall-cladding, mahogany and maple cabinets, and a pietra verde limestone countertop.

West elevation

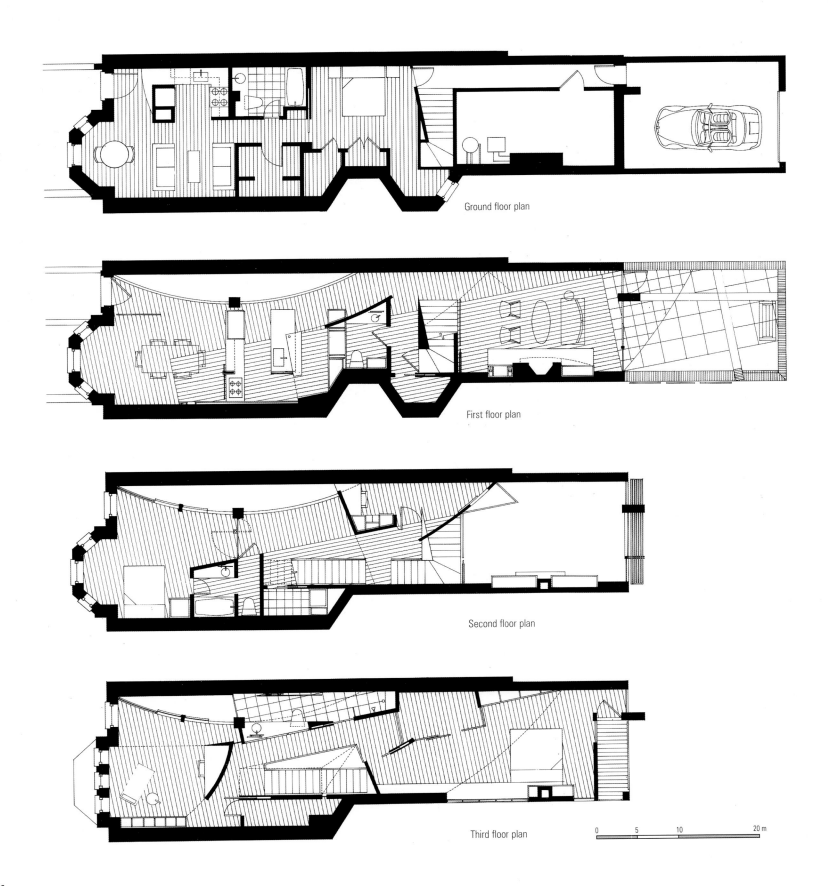

Ground floor plan

First floor plan

Second floor plan

Third floor plan

0   5   10   20 m

MVRDV

Borneo Houses

Amsterdam, The Netherlands

In Borneo (Sporenburg) two dwellings stand out because of their resolution and the great spatial possibilities applied within their limited size.

The first of the dwellings, located on plot 18, is 4.2 meters wide and 16 meters high and has a spacious double-height terrace on the sea-side of the building. Another block suspended over the terrace and the water houses the bedroom and a bathroom. The remaining irregular spaces of the house - kitchen-dining room, living room and study - are linked so as to provide a fluid and simple transition from one room to the next. Different ceiling heights and levels of privacy define the rooms, which are connected to the outside through an exclusive entrance.

On plot 12 a very unusual private dwelling was designed in an experiment to adapt the layout to the narrow site. The result is an alleyway and a house that is only 2.5 meters wide. Breaking with normal practice, the whole length and height of the half that was built along the back street has a glass facade, while the facades facing the street and the channel were left entirely closed. The open facade rotates the house to face the alley, which houses three separate elements: a storage and parking block, a closed volume containing a guest room and bathroom and another closed block adding extra width the studios on the first and second floors. These design solutions allowed an extremely narrow house to be transformed into a sufficiently spacious dwelling.

Photographs: Nicholas Kane

Plot 18

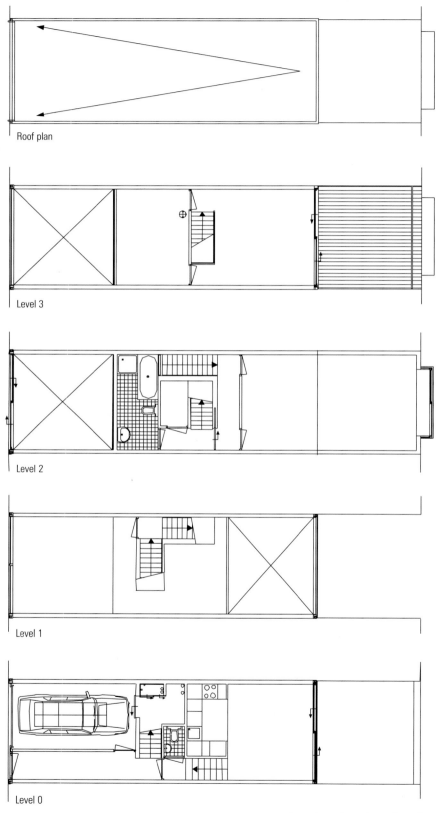

Roof plan

Level 3

Level 2

Level 1

Level 0

Plot 12

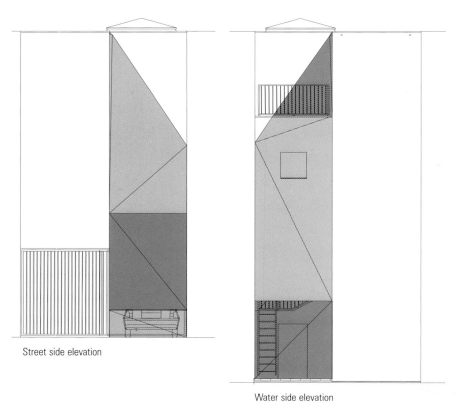

Street side elevation

Water side elevation

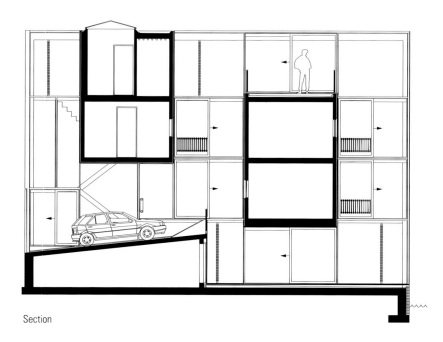

Section

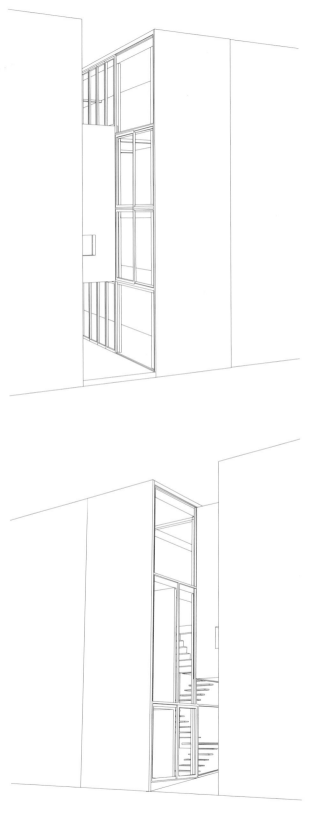

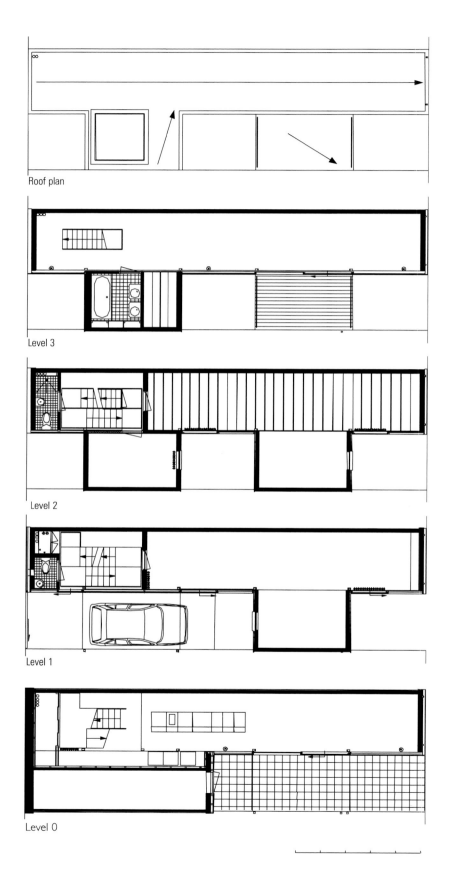

Roof plan

Level 3

Level 2

Level 1

Level 0

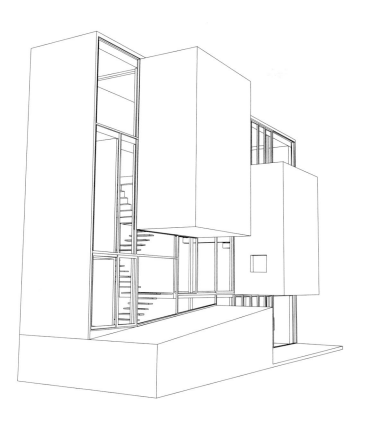

Unlike the neighboring dwellings, because the site was so narrow this house has its fully glazed main facade at the side facing the alley. Modules were added to enlarge the building and give it personality.

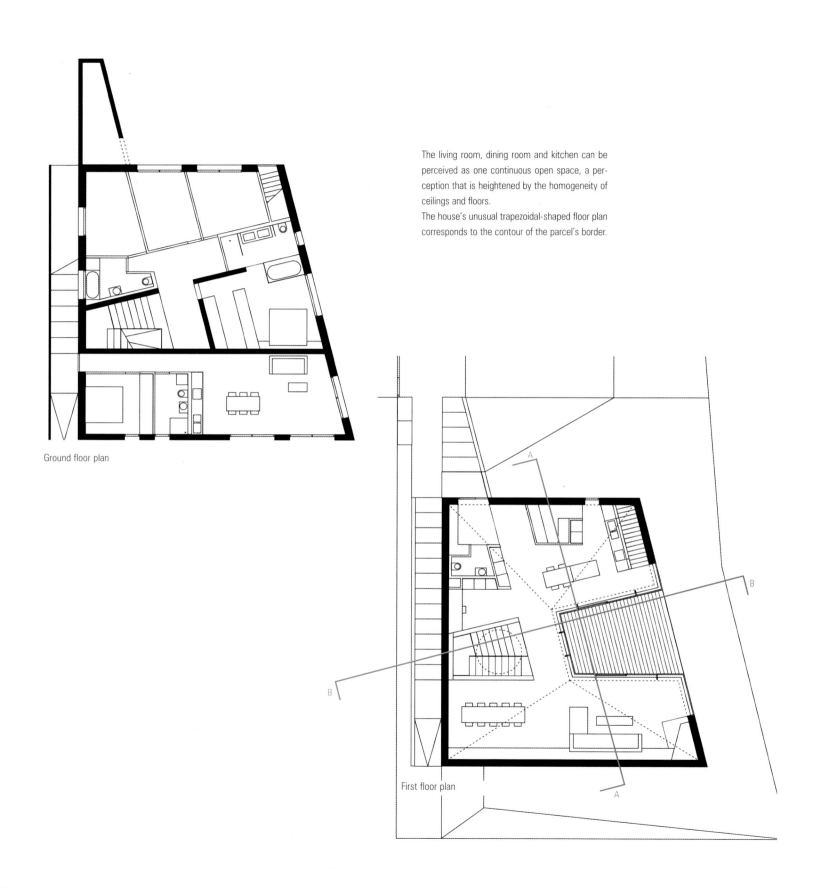

Ground floor plan

The living room, dining room and kitchen can be perceived as one continuous open space, a perception that is heightened by the homogeneity of ceilings and floors.

The house's unusual trapezoidal-shaped floor plan corresponds to the contour of the parcel's border.

First floor plan

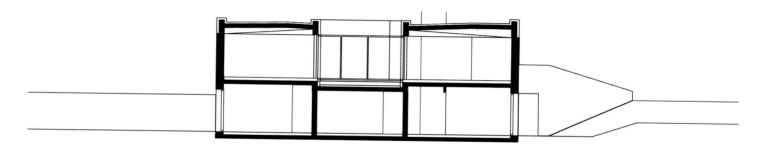

Section AA

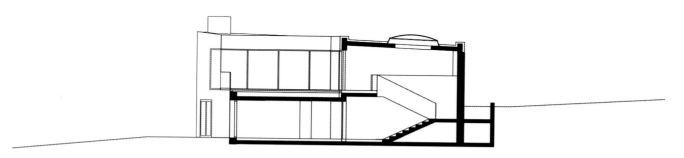

Section BB

The only opening on the south side of the house is a large round skylight, which casts a roaming patch of sunlight onto the floor, which is clad in a light gray glossy epoxy resin, which has been sealed with a seamless finish, giving it a reflective sheen.

Querkraft

SPS one-family detached house

Vienna, Austria

This house is situated on a quiet piece of land with panoramic views over Vienna, orientated towards the southeast. The position in an allotment settlement area (the construction area of max. 50 square meters per building unit) had to be newly and favorably interpreted for a house with an effective area of nearly 300 square meters to be created.

The main building was set into the hillside, as far in the rear of the property as possible to position an optimally large garden area in front of the building. House and garden represent a confluent living unit for over two thirds of the year. The transition from indoors to the outdoor garden is accentuated by a shading device constructed as a scaffolding in a deep terrace area.

Constructing the living spaces dug into the hillside in the form of a cellar made it possible according to the building code to have 83 instead of 50 square meters surface.

The parental bedroom and a second "special" living room have been added on top of the hillside house. The breathtaking panoramic views can be enjoyed daily by the owners on waking up and falling asleep. This floor has been designed in order to have the maximum view without obstructing at the same time the views of the surrounding houses.

Photographs: Querkraft

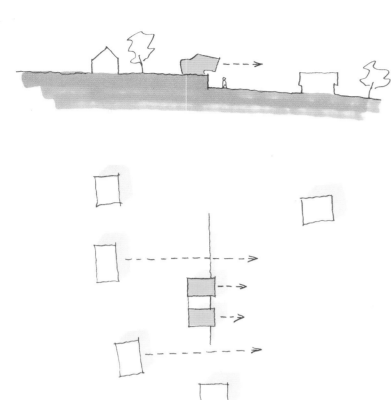

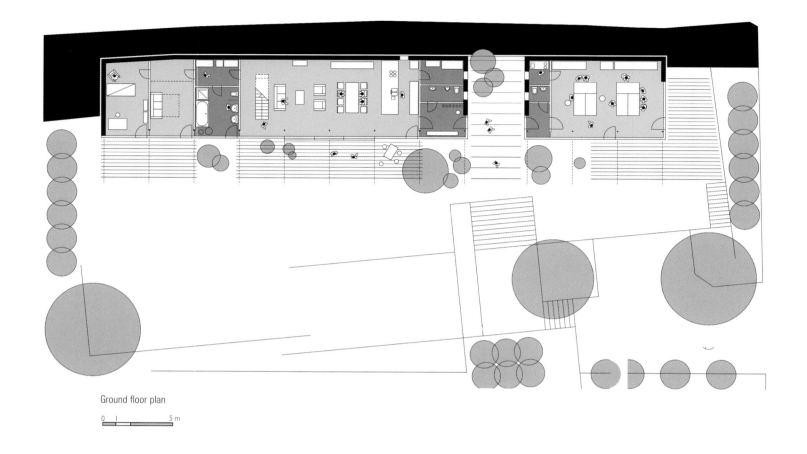

Ground floor plan

0   5 m

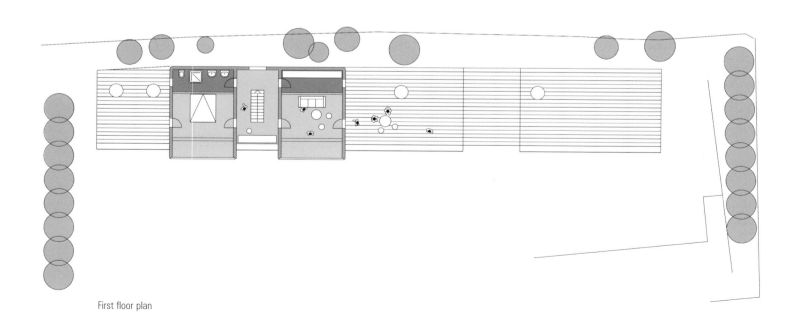

First floor plan

93

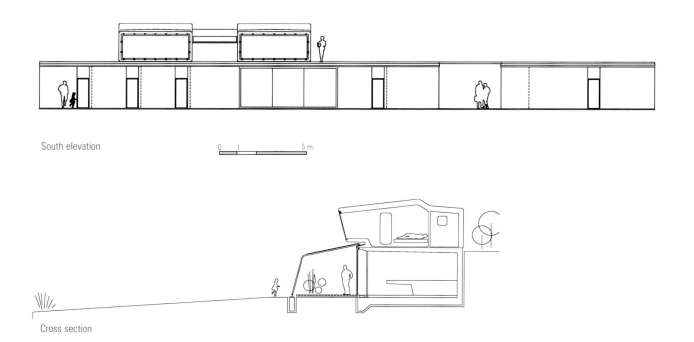

South elevation

0 1   5 m

Cross section

The house is designed so that the gor-
geous views crown and penetrate
everyday life without dominating it.

Monolab Architects
Body House

Rotterdam, The Netherlands

The site of this house is situated in one of three rows of seven houses each, in the Katendrecht residential redevelopment on a harbour pier that was previously part of Rotterdam's China Town. The initial design concept was connecting the kitchen/dining heart of the building to the exterior, which was resolved by developing a wire frame and covering this with a skin to contain service spaces. The building is like a living organism, with its central heart and a faceted eye looking out over the river. The frame is angular, cut like a rough diamond and covered by different types of skins: metal grill, glass and particle sheet with epoxy coating and synthetic fabric.

The Body House is an urban stack of three small projects, with the lower and the upper embodying opposing housing concepts. Below is the fixed, interiorized, dark, heavy base, a cast concrete plinth that is a kind of ground floor basement area. On top is the roof terrace reflecting a campsite with a free, open, light and flexible nylon tent.

In between, a steel cage consisting of a series of columns and beams placed on the plinth defines the living area. The steel structure of the body stabilises the whole building, carrying part of the concrete floor with its foot and connected to the roof beams at the top, and pushing out the big window towards the panoramic river view. Four types of openings physically connect the body to the outside: a pivoting entry slab, a flip door to the patio, a tilting plank to the terrace and a shifting tablet to the roof.

Photographs: MONOLAB Architects

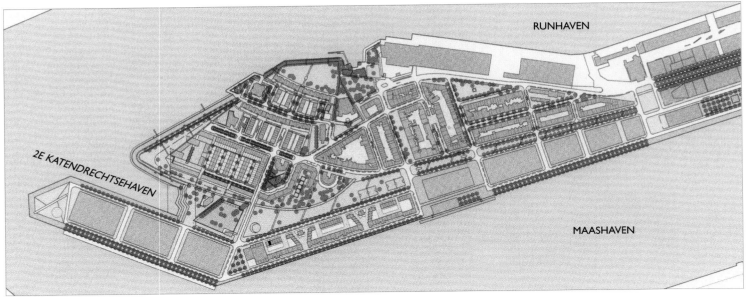

Site plan

The Body House is an urban stack of three small projects: a solid, opaque concrete base below, an open, light roof terrace with a flexible nylon tent above, and the body in the living area in-between.

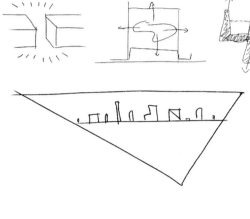

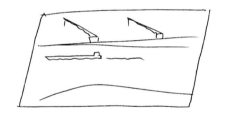

The building is like a living organism, with its central heart and a faceted eye looking out over the river. The body wire frame is angular, cut like a rough diamond, connecting the different parts of the building, from the concrete base to the roof and the large window that is the main feature of the facade.

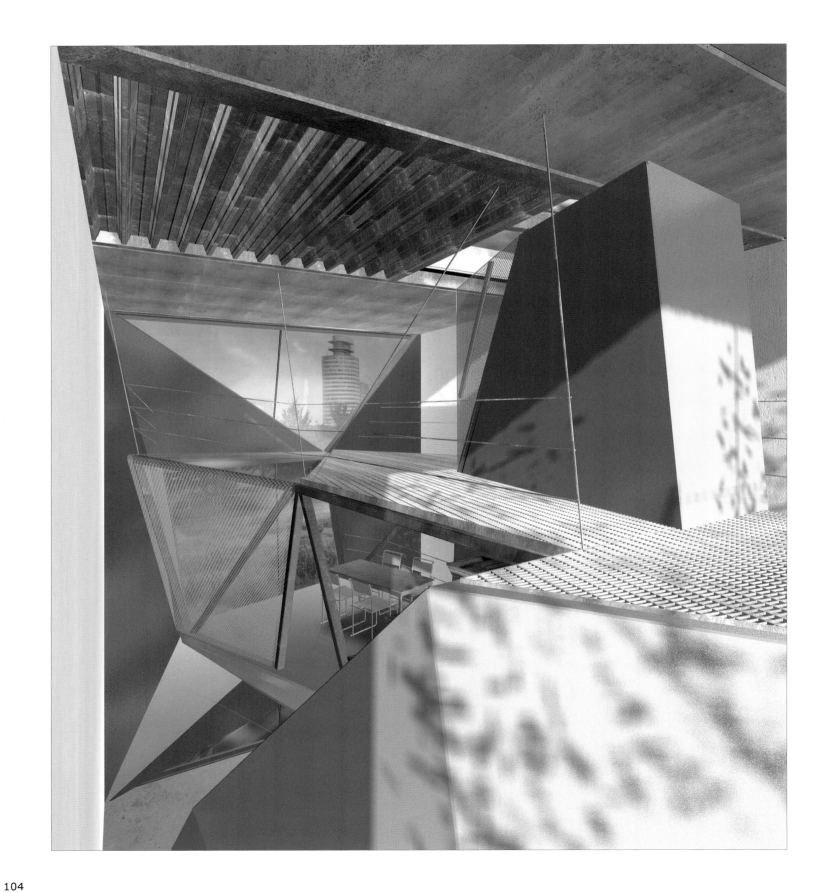

Breakdown of the three different elements that structure the house: the concrete base, the wire frame body and the steel cage with the flexible roof tent on top.

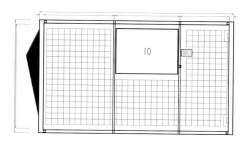

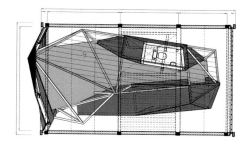

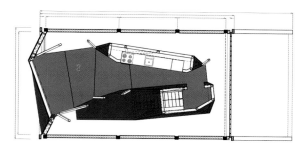

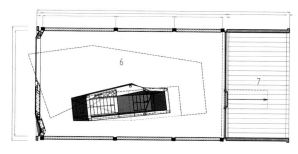

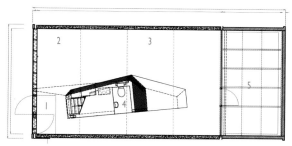

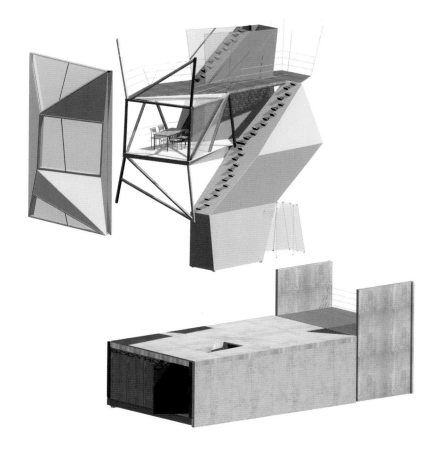

1. Entry
2. Storage
3. Bedroom
4. Bathroom
5. Patio
6. Living
7. Terrace
8. Dining / kitchen
9. Transparent floor
10. Roof terrace

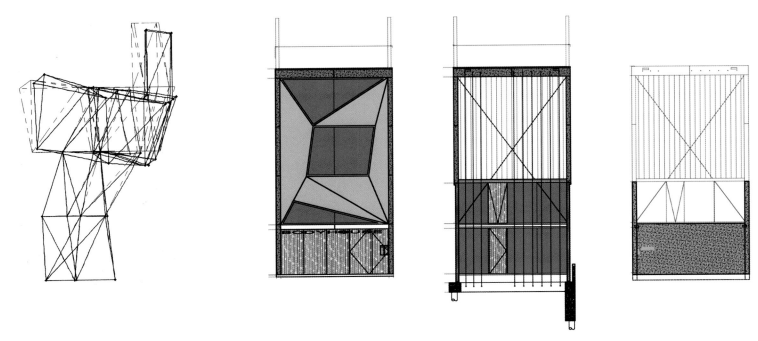

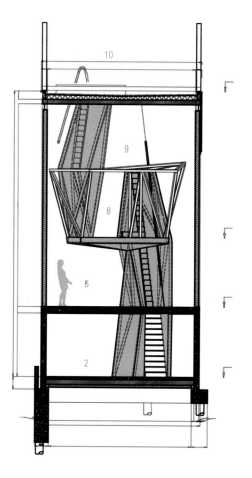

1. Entry
2. Storage
3. Bedroom
4. Bathroom
5. Patio
6. Living
7. Terrace
8. Dining / kitchen
9. Transparent floor
10. Roof terrace

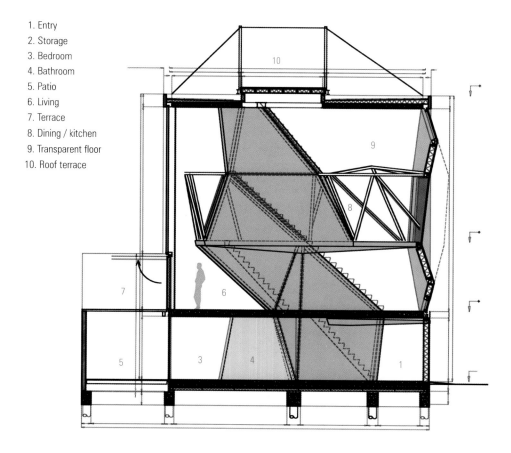

Sugiura Office
House H

Nagoya, Japan

House H is located in a narrow site surrounded by neighboring buildings. In Japan, this configuration is known as "Unagi no Nedoko" or "the nest of an eel", and it is common in traditional city-house districts in Kyoto, presenting special privacy and space problems for new buildings. This particular site is open to the north, where there is a busy road. The clients wanted to avoid having windows looking out to the road, but they still hoped to have a bright and open house.

Within this narrow site, the architects placed the volume leaving a 2.5 m strip of land to the south and a 1 m strip to the east. These spaces are used to help guide the light and air to the interior in order to create an open feeling inside.

The largest openings were placed on the south side to allow as much direct sunlight as possible into the building. Frosted glass for diffused light was placed on the east-facing side of the first floor. On the western side where there is no setback at all from the neighbors, skylights were designed to allow the light to filter through the roof and floor down to the first floor. At the northern end of the second floor, a kind of chimney acts as a vent to allow air to flow from the south to the north. The resulting space manages to have free flowing air and three different types of light - direct, diffused and changing light - to create a house that feels open.

The structure was designed to take up minimum space. Although it is actually a hybrid that uses both frames and Vierendeel structures, to the observer it appears like a simple box.

Photographs: Tamoutsu Kurumada

The type of narrow site surrounded by neighboring buildings is called "Unagi no Nedoko" or "the nest of an eel" in Japan. The house avoids opening out to the busy street in front, with light entering mainly from the southern and western sides.

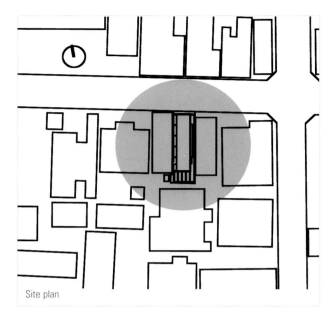

Site plan

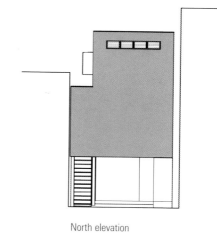

North elevation

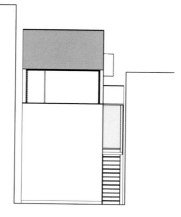

South elevation

111

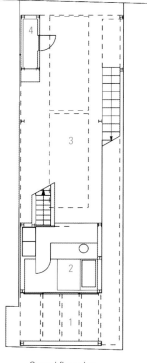

Ground floor plan

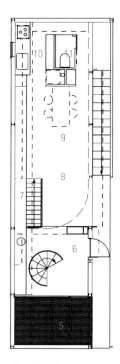

First floor plan

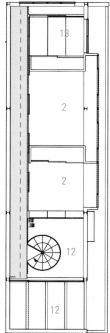

Second floor plan

1. Court
2. Bedroom
3. Parking
4. Storage
5. Terrace
6. Entrance
7. Counter
8. Living
9. Dining
10. Kitchen
11. Lavatory
12. Void
13. Tatami room

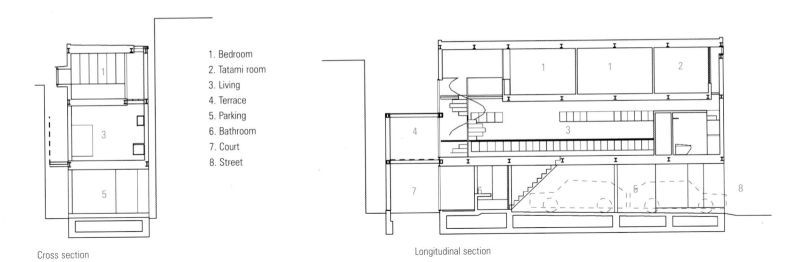

Cross section

1. Bedroom
2. Tatami room
3. Living
4. Terrace
5. Parking
6. Bathroom
7. Court
8. Street

Longitudinal section

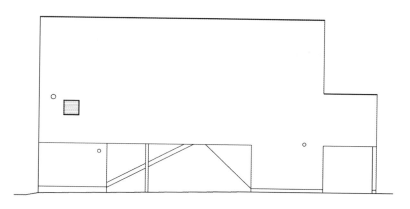

West elevation

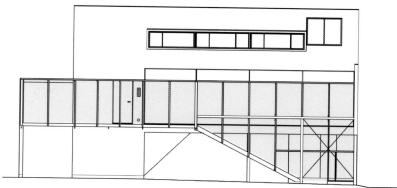

East elevation

The warm redwood timber contrasts with stainless steel details in these two houses built on a subdivided corner block. Irregularly shaped windows frame the surrounding environment, including a cathedral on the opposite corner.

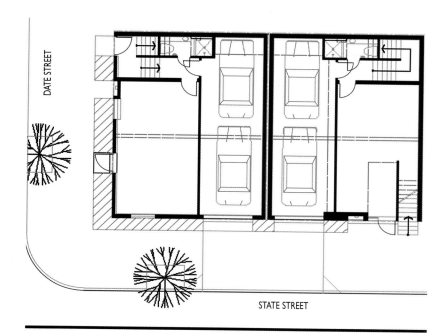

DATE STREET

STATE STREET

Ground floor plan

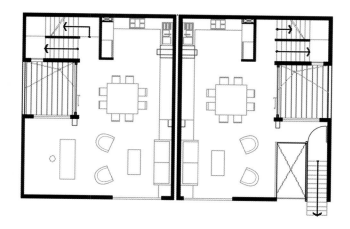

First floor plan

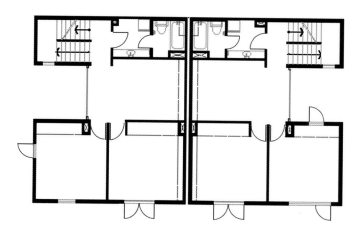

Second floor plan

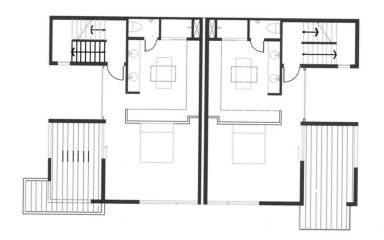

Third floor plan

Inside, simple peaceful spaces are created using high quality materials such as dark stained oak cabinets, clear maple floors and red velvet curtains.

Norisada Maeda

The Rose

Tokyo, Japan

The design for The Rose was based on the idea of 'scooping out volumes from a potted pudding with a soon'. This process was used to impose a geometric transformation on a regular cubic building, resulting in the emergence of a spatial 'obverse and reverse'.

The side that is perceived visually and continuously from the outside is the 'obverse' or concave side, while the other side is the 'reverse' or convex side. Obverse is not necessarily exterior and reverse is not necessarily interior in this building that transverses the idea of an interior/exterior in architecture.

Rather than dividing space through a two-dimensional layout, the space is segmented by carving out a volume of air with an R-shaped concrete frame. Although it seems contradictory, space is developed in The Rose through depth that is related to the surface layer, which does not necessarily mean the facade or a regular interior setting. The usual floor-wall-ceiling distinctions disappear, and the living spaces were only named after the house was built.

The building could be considered civil engineering rather than architecture, focusing on surface. The architect interprets 'surface' as something rooted in the systematic theory of a creative attitude, and the house as an organism which simultaneously calls on the consciousness.

Photographs: Nacása & Partners

128

The house is conceived as volumes carved out of a regular cubic building. A spatial 'obverse and reverse' emerges, with concave and convex surfaces replacing the usual concepts of interior and exterior.

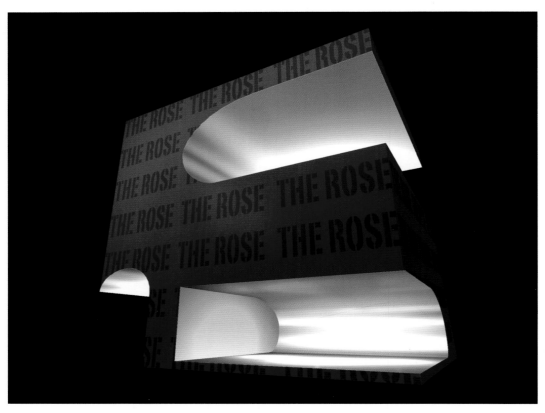

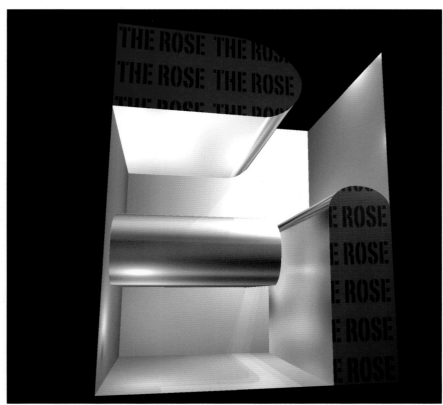

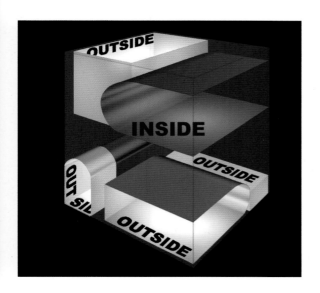

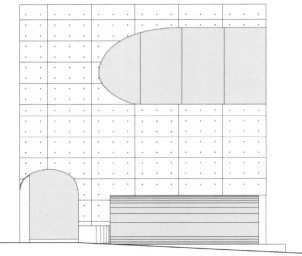

West elevation

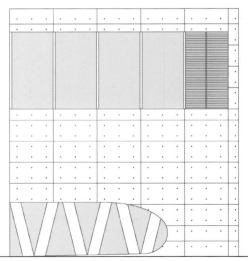

South elevation

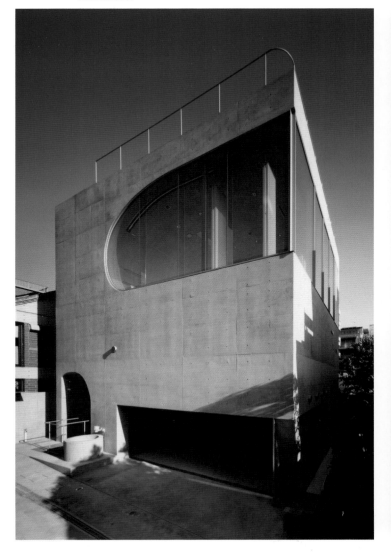

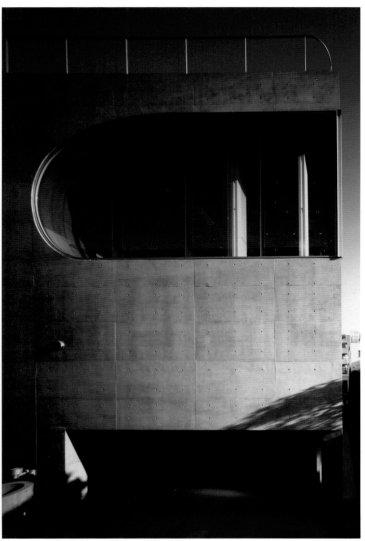

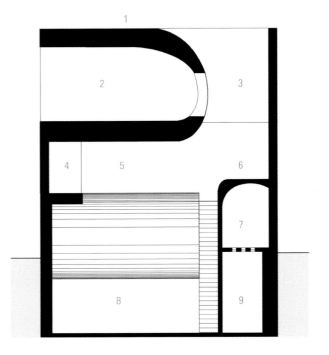

SECTION "A"

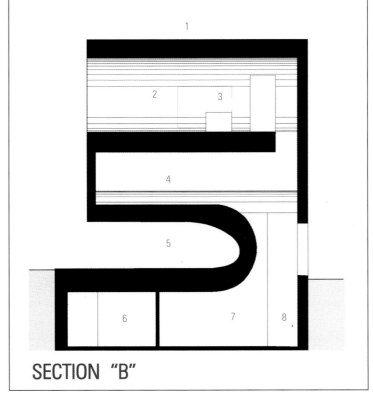

SECTION "A"

1. Roof
2. Living room
3. Garden
4. Bathroom
5. Bedroom
6. Work space
7. Entrance
8. Bedroom
9. Guest bedroom

SECTION "B"

1. Roof
2. Living room
3. Kitchen
4. Bedroom
5. Parking area
6. Workout room
7. Bedroom
8. Garden

SECTION "B"

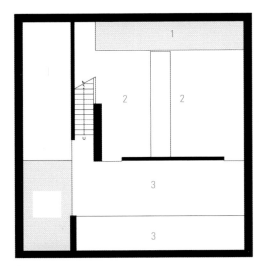

Basement
1. Garden
2. Bedroom
3. Storage

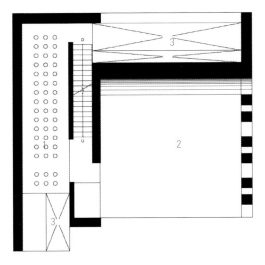

Ground floor
1. Entrance
2. Parking area
3. Void

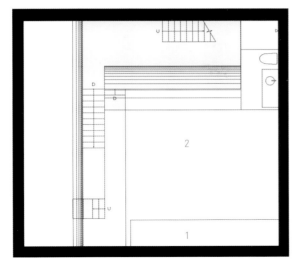

First floor
1. Bedroom
2. Storage

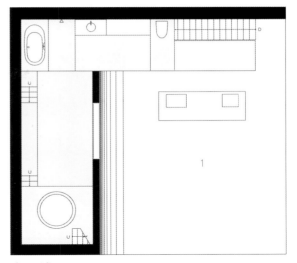

Second floor
1. Living room

Rather than dividing space through a two-dimensional layout, the space is segmented by carving out a volume of air with an R-shaped concrete frame. These concave living spaces are rooted in an original conception of space related to volume and surface.

Eugeen Liebaut

Verhaeghe House

Sint Pieters Leeuw, Belgium

The program for this house near Brussels was chosen from among ten competing architectural studios. The Verhaeghe house is a simple two-story structure with a flat roof, hemmed in on both sides by neighboring buildings. Since the site itself was seven meters wide and zoning restrictions would only allow a height of six meters, a modest volume had to be designed. With such spatial restrictions, the architects decided to make room by sinking the ground floor 80cm to the level of the foundation masonry. Financially, this is a simple enough operation; while the advantages gained in spatial configuration are highly attractive.

The living room is a high-ceilinged, transparent space. Here, the inhabitants move freely about between two strategically-placed volumes - the kitchen and the toilet - which do not reach the full height of the ceiling. Together, these volumes form a screen of sorts within the transparent volume which provides the necessary privacy from the public street. The high and wide glass facade rises from an incision between the volume and the socle like a rare and floating object.

The rear facade is also entirely glazed, making the steel-grated terrace outside seem like a continuation of the dwelling. By working with grates, the bedrooms on the ground floor are ensured sufficient light. This relatively small house enjoys a spatiality which many a majestic villa can only dream of.

Photographs: Saskia Vanderstichele

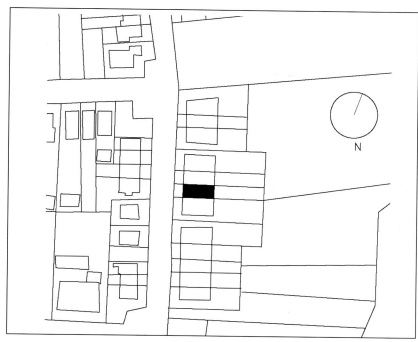

Site plan

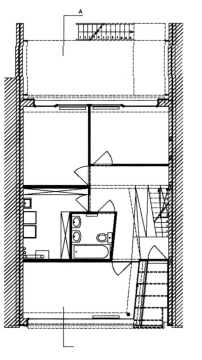

Ground floor plan

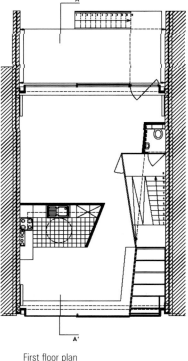

First floor plan

Since zoning restrictions required a height of no more than 6 meters, interior space was gained by sinking the house by nearly one meter.
The block containing the kitchen is positioned to shield the interior from views from the street.

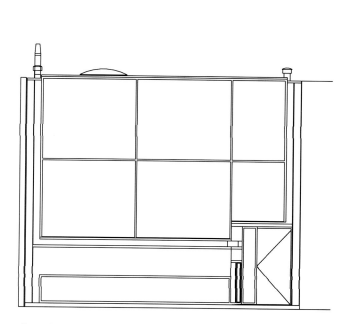

Front elevation

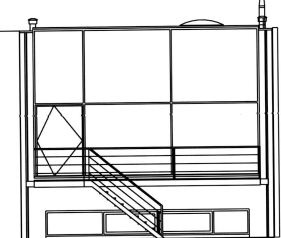

Back elevation

Jahn Associates Architects
Grant House

Sydney, Australia

The Grant House is located in the back streets of inner city Sydney, where rows of terrace houses are separated by small-scale industrial warehouses. The original exterior brick walls have been retained, acting as an apron to the layers of timber and steel that make up the new facade. Two of the pine trusses from the original building have been reused in the first floor living area. Entry is through the outer brick skin and is marked by a galvanized steel lintel plate.

The idea of the home as a sanctuary in the city is central to the design, defining the organization of the spaces within the building and their materiality. The house is stacked to the south, enabling a ground-level, north-facing courtyard to emerge. Situated within this tranquil and contemplative space is the timber-clad studio, designed as a workspace and meditation room.

It is placed to take advantage of the courtyard's water feature as well as providing a visual and physical link with the street entry.

The interior spaces are calm and protective, wrapping around the courtyard, and designed to accommodate an extensive art collection, as well as its future expansion.

The interior play of spatial relationships and materials in conjunction with the folded planes of the exterior, which wrap the surface of the building through its successive skins, unite to both embrace the life of the city and shun it.

In addition, the simplicity of the new volume brings a new dimension to the street and encourages interaction through the natural aging of the materials, the original brick shell acting as the catalyst for an inventive and human response to the experience of living in the city.

Photographs: Brett Boardman and Ghaham Jahn

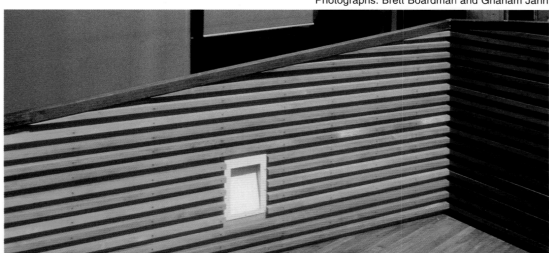

The house is stacked to the south, enabling a ground level, north-facing courtyard to emerge. The courtyard allows for natural day lighting of the interior, controlled by operable aluminum louvers on the ground floor to screen the lower bedrooms.

150

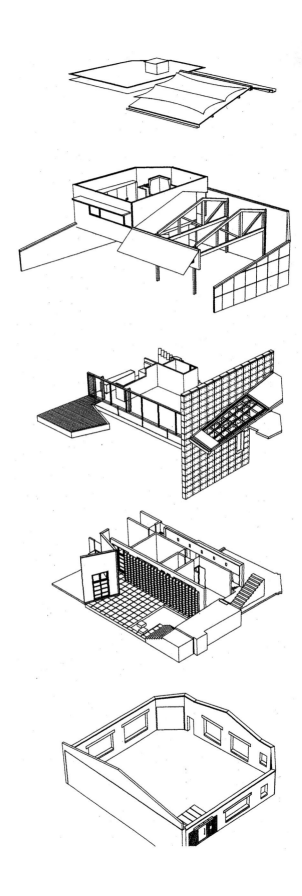

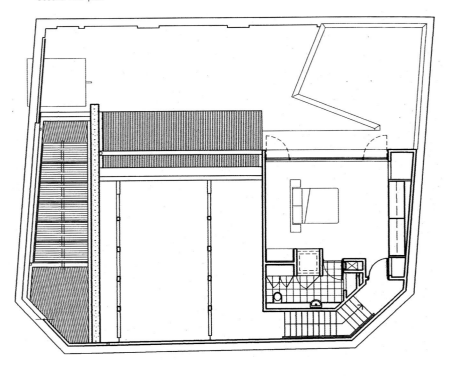

The uppermost floor accommodates the master bedroom, revealed on the exterior as a horizontal layer of corrugated metal sheeting, a material often seen cladding the impromptu lean-to structures attached to nearby terraces.

First floor plan

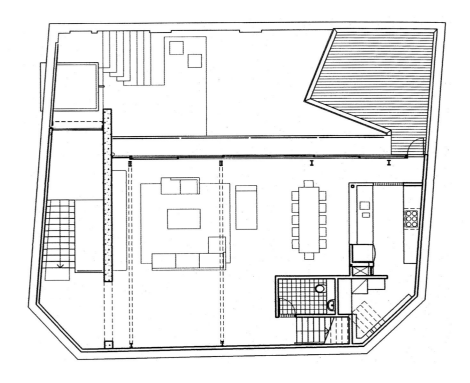

154

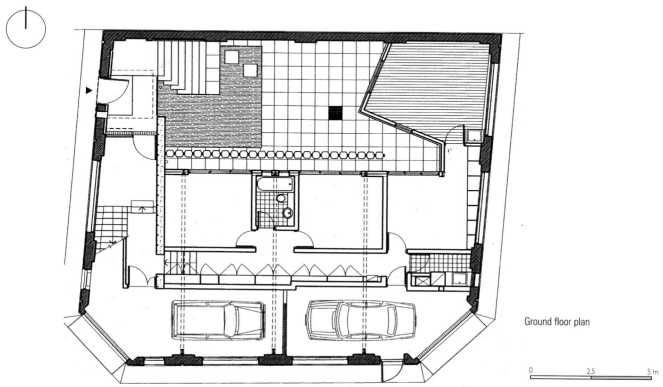

Ground floor plan

0   2,5   5 m

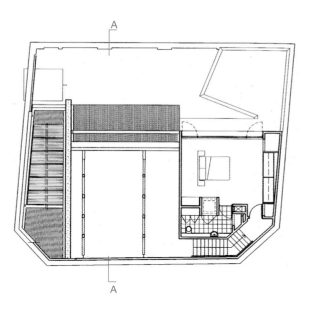

AA Section

	RL 49.10
1	
2	RL 48.80
3	RL 45.70
4	RL 43.00
5	RL 40.80
6	RL 40.43
7	RL 39.80
8	RL 39.30

0   2,5   5 m

1. Second floor roof
2. First floor roof
3. Second floor master bedroom
4. First floor living

5. Raper St. entry
6. Ground floor
7. Studio floor
8. Existing ground floor

Georges Maurios
Montenegro House

Paris, France

The architect, originally reticent to take on this project because of spatial and budgetary restrictions, was eventually seduced by the unique challenge that it offered. The 7x12-meter plot of land was hemmed in tightly between two party walls and, at the back, there was a 4.5-meter-high, south-facing separating wall which had to be retained. Furthermore, the derelict framework of an abandoned construction was still on the site.

In spite of the setbacks, a spacious four-story home was achieved. A maximum of volume and floor area was capitalized on by the use of very economical and technically improved materials such as steel, wood and sandwich panels. Many of the elements were prefabricated off-site, transported in and simply pieced together. The structure was fairly lightweight and therefore did not require a complex and expensive foundation.

The ground plan of the house consists of two distinct parts: on one side a 2-meter-wide strip accommodates the staircase, kitchen, laundry, and all of the bathrooms and toilets, while the other side (5 meters wide) consists of living areas, a lounge, bedrooms and a studio.

The living room, part of which is double height, is connected to the kitchen and the stairwell so that it forms the dwelling's spatial center and occupies the entire first floor. It is extended outside onto the wooden terrace overlooking one end of a narrow garden.

The entire structure is based on steel columns and beams. The skeleton is visible on the inside, where it complements the overall industrial feel of the house. The floors have been made from 140mm-thick galvanized steel panels, which are also in tune with the aesthetic quality of the whole building as well as enhancing the acoustic quality of the individual spaces. The walls and the roof are clad in insulated steel panels.

Photographs: Gaston & Jean-Marie Monthiers

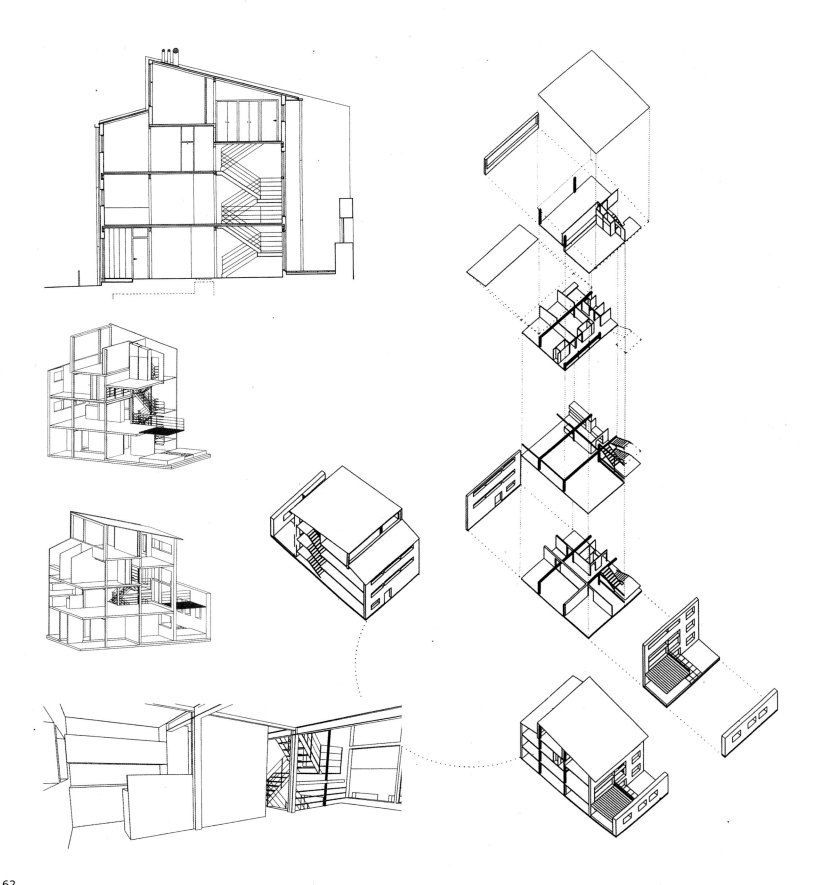

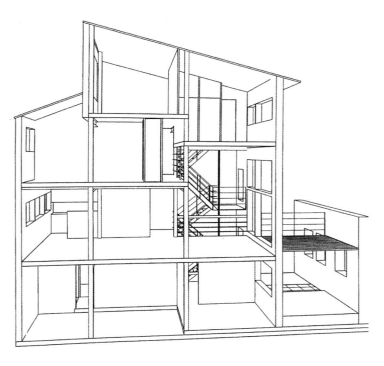

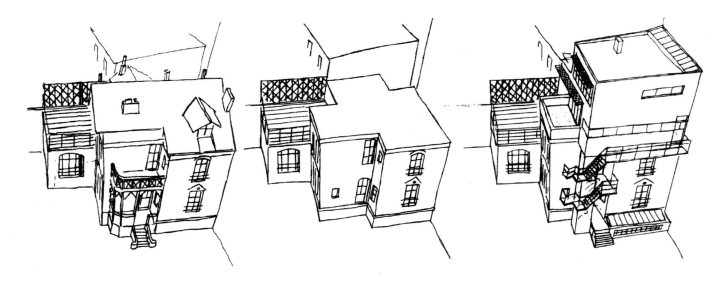

The interior presents a unified aesthetic scheme, including exposed steel beams, a seemingly "unfinished" and industrialized ceiling and an open-plan, galvanized steel staircase and railings. In the same vein, perfect finishes for floor and walls were avoided.

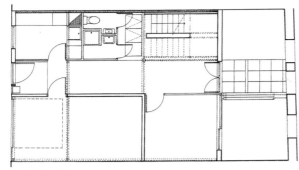

Ground floor plan

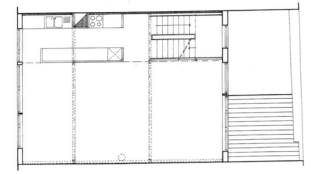

First floor plan

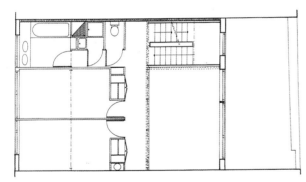

Second floor plan

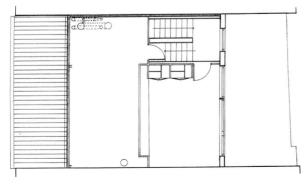

Third floor plan

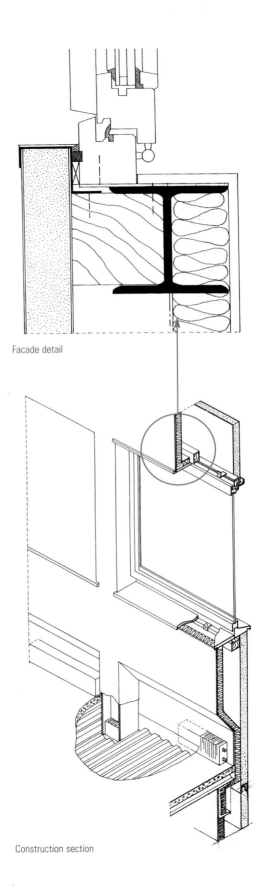

Facade detail

Construction section

Christoph Mayrhofer

Single Family House Machly/Schwarz

Mautern, Austria

This single-family house is situated in Mautern, a small town in the region of "Wachau" a famous winegrowing area, about 60 kilometers west of Vienna. The building site is located just about 300 meters from the river Danube.

Origially the owners, two teachers at the local highschool, were just looking for a factory-built house selected from a catalogue, but for one or the other reason were not satisfied with the choice on offer. Finally they sought an architect's advice and collaborated with him during the design process. They wanted a house with a large space for books, working and reading areas, with much space for living, cooking, listening to music and all the other things one needs to feel good.

To keep as much free space as possible, the architect decided to design a strung-out building running north to south, self-contained like a tube, with large openings at each end and one in the middle to the west, where it opens to the ter-race and the garden. While the main house is a timber-construction towards the street a one-storey concrete structure containing the carport and a guestroom stands at right angles, assuring privacy and shelter to the terrace and the garden behind. Where the "tube" ascends, hovering above the concrete base below, there is the li-brary with more than four thousand books. At the opposite end is the living room with a large window. Below the living room, with descending ground, the basement becomes an additional liv-ing room with an exit to a small terrace. The third terrace is connected to the library-level, a hover-ing metallic wing that extends beyond the guestroom below. Together with a largely open and flowing interior the house forms a coherent space on different levels, climbing and plunging down, opening and closing in, bringing the out-doors inside and extending the indoors outside: the house as landscape within the landscape.

Photographs: Hertha Hurnaus

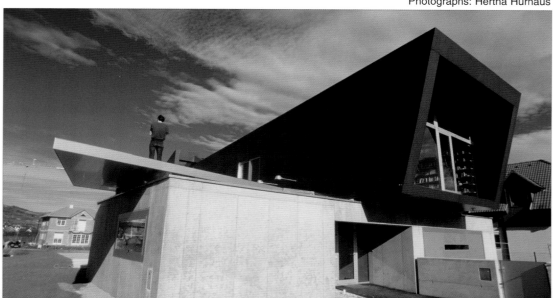

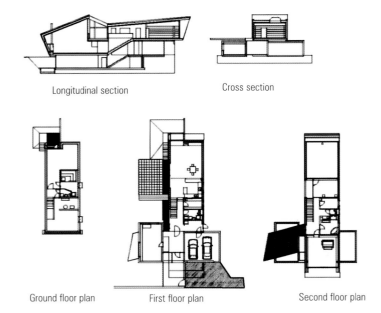

Longitudinal section

Cross section

Ground floor plan

First floor plan

Second floor plan

The site presented a contradictory image with an amazing scenery with vineyards both at the north and the south while the immediate neighborhood was a faceless zone on the fringes of the small town with a jumble of single family houses and apartment blocks of bad quality.

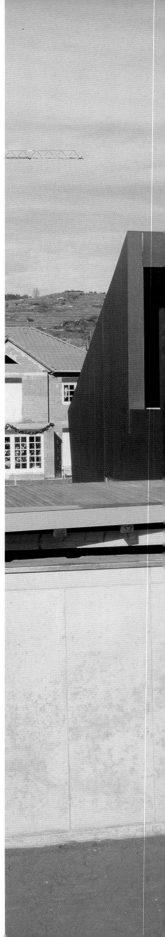

Kunihide Oshinomi & Takesi Semba

Timber Frame House with a Curtain Wall

Shinagawa-ku, Tokyo, Japan

The ideas governing the structural design of this four-story house derive from having seen the tragic spectacle of the destruction of timber houses in the Kobe earthquake and as a result of a close collaboration between the architects and a structural engineer specializing in high-rise buildings.

The site for this project was of an irregular, truncated triangle shape. A retaining wall was on the side by the boundary wall and timber was on the other side.

The bearing strength of the ground was not sufficient for concrete construction and, because of fire safety regulations, a steel frame construction would have required fire-proof cladding. Yet, if timber-panel construction had been chosen, it would have been difficult to make large openings.

Amid such constraints, the framework that was decided upon was a semi-rigid structure of reinforced concrete, glue-laminated timber frame with metal fittings, and a wooden bearing wall.

In order to keep the north and east sides open to the site's more attractive views, the bearing walls are placed on the south and west faces. The north face, now free of cumbersome structural elements, is a curtain wall with double glazing of clear float glass.

Also, by pre-cutting the glue-laminated wood and providing metal joint fittings, a very precise and unrestricted structure was created, while also cutting down on construction time.

In the interior, Japanese beech flooring with a urethane-coat finish creates a cozy atmosphere.

Photographs: Nacása & Partners

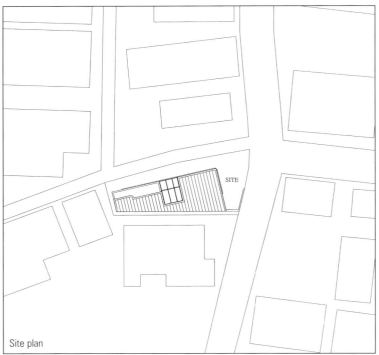

Site plan

The floor-to-ceiling openings on the rear facade are made with cicuta wood.

As a second skin there are small balconies with metal grid floors and aluminium blinds. These act as climatic protection and establish a point of contrast with the wooden frames.

Taku Sakaushi / O.F.D.A.
Zigzag Rooms

Tokyo, Japan

Privacy was a principal concern for this house for two families in the center of Tokyo, built on a site adjacent to a planned seven story building. In order to ensure privacy, the architect designed a trapezoid-shaped plan that allowed the house to look away from the larger residential building.

The exterior zigzag shape that gives the house its name is a combination of alternating windows and walls, where the walls face the residential building and the windows face the south garden. The large, floor to ceiling windows allow natural light into the interior, creating a feeling of openness in the midst of a densely populated area.

The structure of the house consists of reinforced concrete flat slabs, earthquake-resistant walls and more than 30 steel columns. The columns are very slender 70 x 70 mm square bars. These were used because the joints on each end act as hinges which do not bend and can be placed inside the thickness of the walls, according to the position of the walls on each floor.

Photographs: Hiroshi Ueda

The trapezoid-shaped plan is an ingenious solution to the problem of privacy posed by the site. It allows the house to make the best of the garden, and provides the zigzag shaped facade that gives it its name.

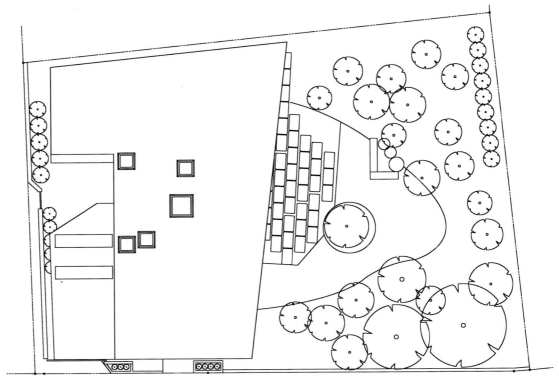

Site plan

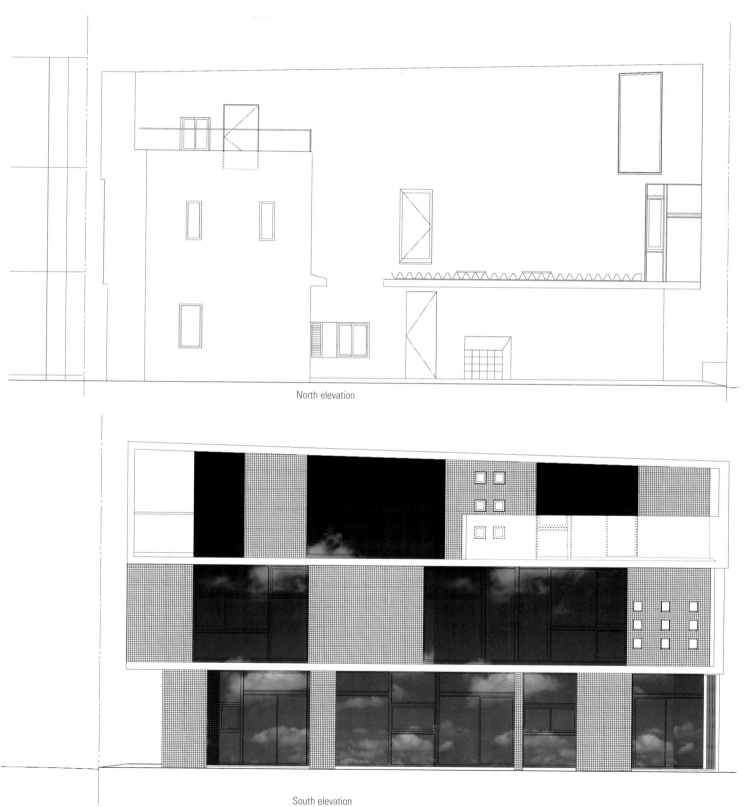

North elevation

South elevation

East elevation

West elevation

The many large windows allow light into the interior during the day and their orientation isolates the house from the surrounding residential buildings.

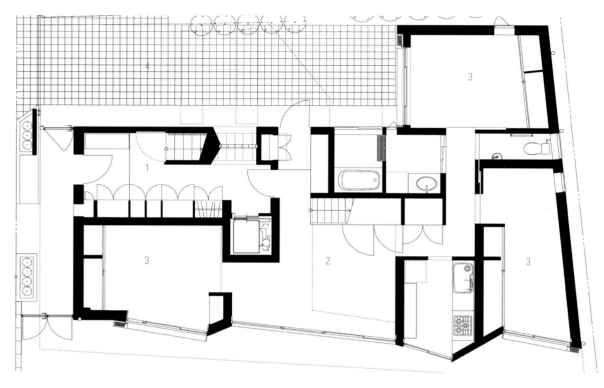

Ground floor plan
1. Entrance
2. Living room
3. Room
4. Garage

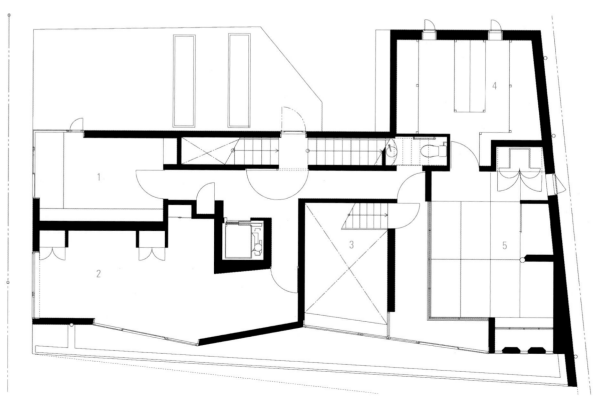

First floor plan
1. Study
2. Music room
3. Void
4. Storage
5. Japanese room

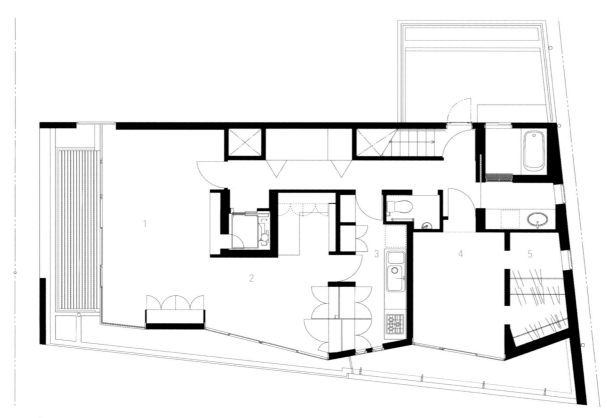

Second floor plan
1. Living room
2. Dining room
3. Kitchen
4. Bedroom
5. Storage

The strong, flexible structural system provides varied interior spaces throughout the
three story house, which has generous garden views.

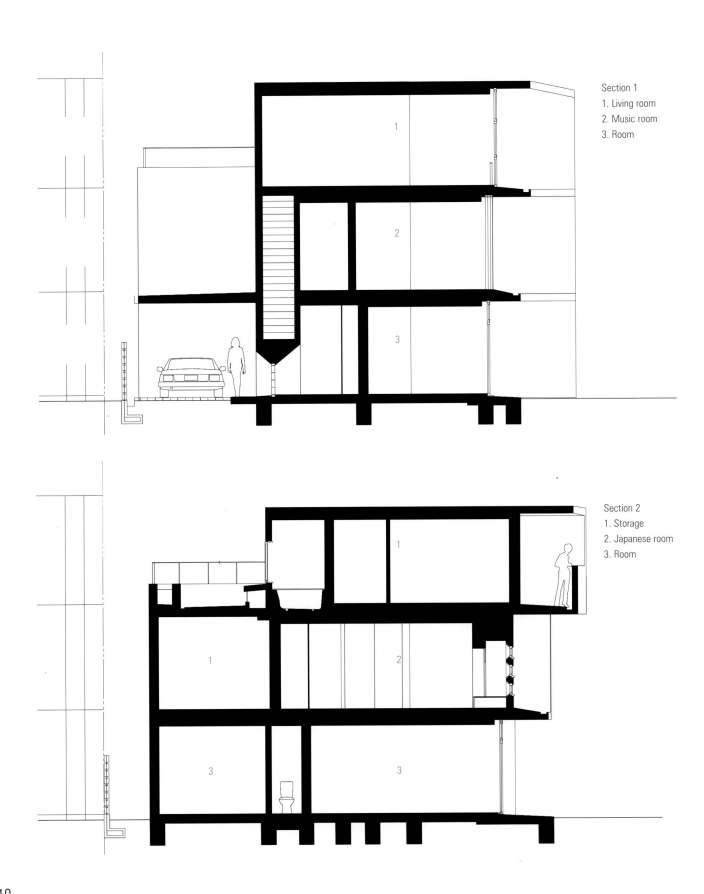

Section 1
1. Living room
2. Music room
3. Room

Section 2
1. Storage
2. Japanese room
3. Room

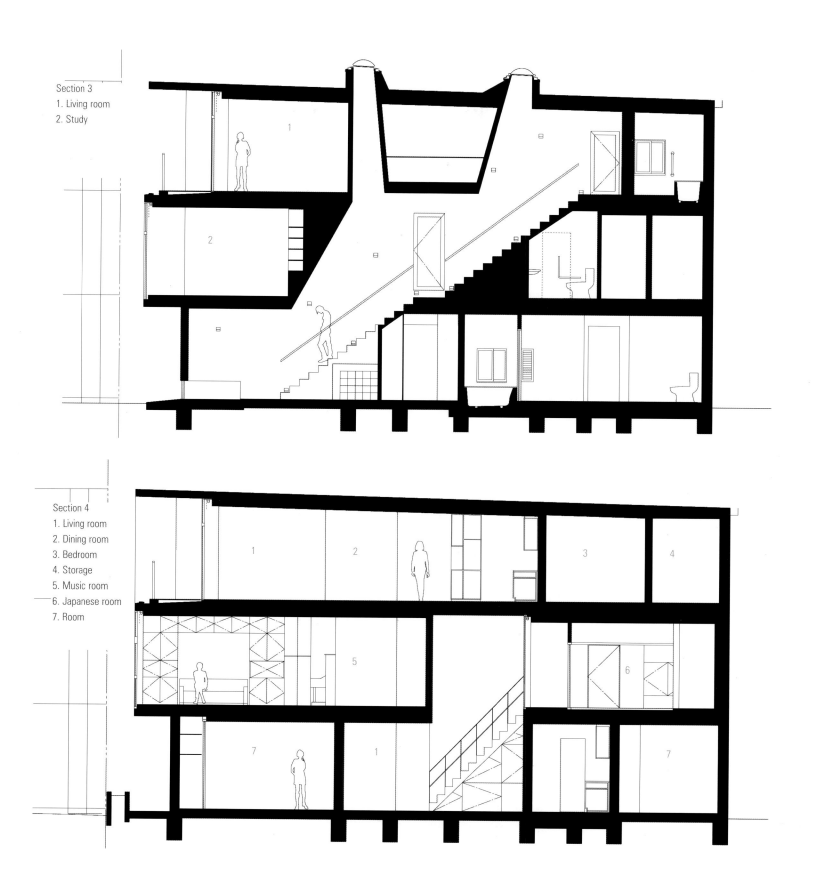

Section 3
1. Living room
2. Study

Section 4
1. Living room
2. Dining room
3. Bedroom
4. Storage
5. Music room
6. Japanese room
7. Room

structure diagram

Figure 1
Where there are no columns,
the flat slabs become very
thick and heavy.

Figure 2

Where steel columns have
been placed, the flat slabs
become slender with a
thickness of 200mm.

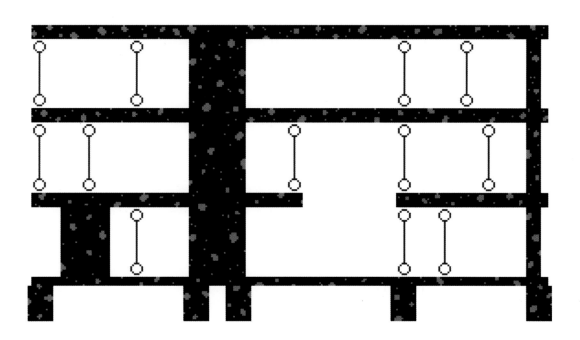

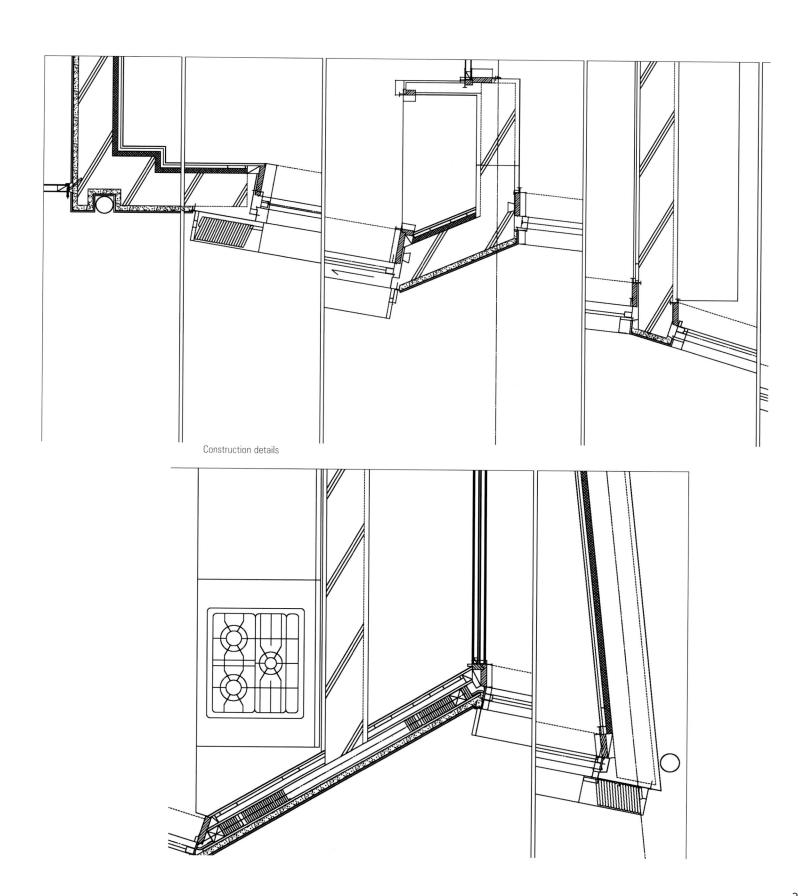

Construction details

213

Manuel Herz

"Legal / Illegal"

Cologne, Germany

This building is the result of a developer's reluctant decision to use architecture to add value to his investment in a complex historical and regulatory context in the city of Bayenthal. The 5.5 x 25 m site, together with heritage, planning and safety regulations, set the conditions for a very clearly defined and unambiguous volume, a transparent orthogonal building set one meter back from the street. As a full construction covering the whole site was not allowed, the volume is reduced by terraces on each level that step down the rear of the building.

In contrast to this "legal" volume conditioned by regulations, there is a second "defiant" volume, a non-orthogonal, free-formed body that exceeds the maximum permitted floor area. It is mainly opaque and traces a path from street level through the heritage-listed gate, moving up and through the floors, with its main mass at the upper levels facing back down the street. It's

windows, goggle-eyed, look into the sky, onto the terraces and down onto the street. Every surface of its faceted volume throws a "shadow area" onto one of the neighboring sites, its irregular shape allowing it to disregard the corresponding regulations and to encroach on the municipal building line on the street. Not a single exterior wall is perpendicular, and the distinctions between wall, floor and ceilings are blurred.

The volume is covered with a red polyutherane coating with allows for a "construction without details" and forms a continuous skin over all surfaces of the building.

By creating a building that combines a volume which respects legal requirements and a second, disrespectful volume, a foreign element is introduced into the urban fabric. The building attempts to enrich its context and express the area's historical and present problems by pushing the limits architecturally.

Photographs: Boris Becker

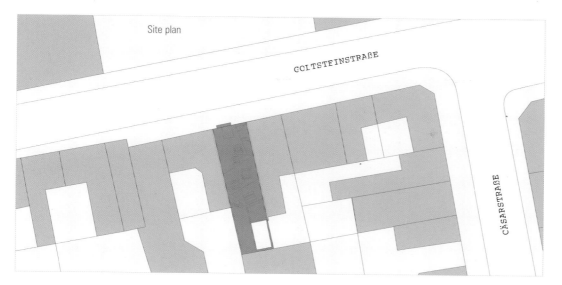

Site plan

COLTSTEINSTRAßE

CÄSARSTRAßE

This new building is set on a narrow site measuring 5.5 x 25 meters in the historical district of the city. Its construction was subject to strict norms governing the heritage of the site, norms which the architects adhered to on the lower volume, but violated on the upper.

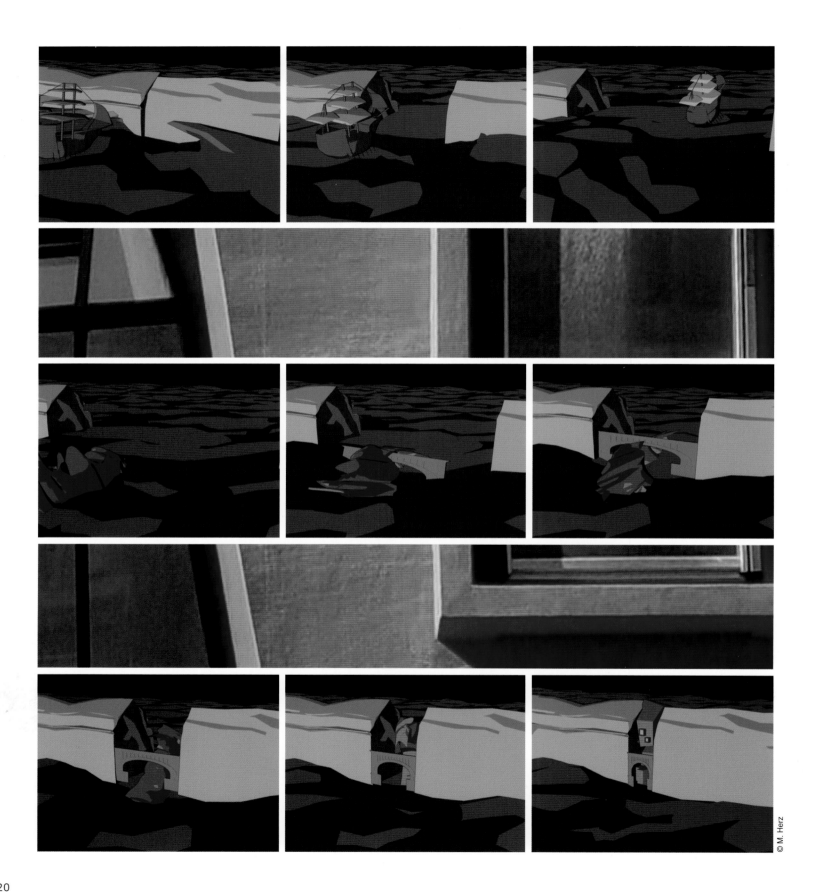

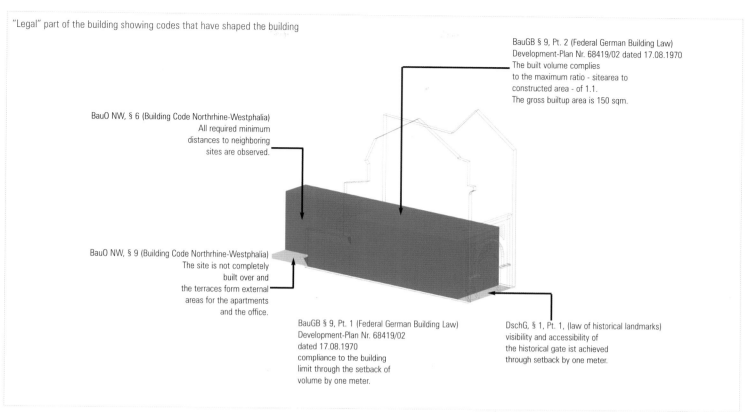

"Legal" part of the building showing codes that have shaped the building

BauGB § 9, Pt. 2 (Federal German Building Law)
Development-Plan Nr. 68419/02 dated 17.08.1970
The built volume complies
to the maximum ratio - sitearea to
constructed area - of 1.1.
The gross builtup area is 150 sqm.

BauO NW, § 6 (Building Code Northrhine-Westphalia)
All required minimum
distances to neighboring
sites are observed.

BauO NW, § 9 (Building Code Northrhine-Westphalia)
The site is not completely
built over and
the terraces form external
areas for the apartments
and the office.

BauGB § 9, Pt. 1 (Federal German Building Law)
Development-Plan Nr. 68419/02
dated 17.08.1970
compliance to the building
limit through the setback of
volume by one meter.

DschG, § 1, Pt. 1, (law of historical landmarks)
visibility and accessibility of
the historical gate ist achieved
through setback by one meter.

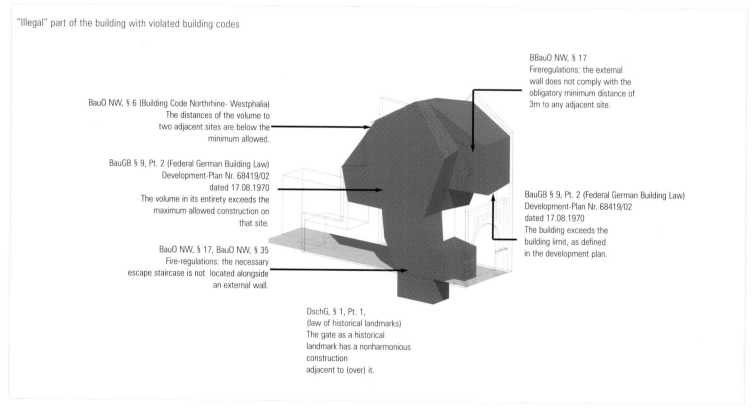

"Illegal" part of the building with violated building codes

BBauO NW, § 17
Fireregulations: the external
wall does not comply with the
obligatory minimum distance of
3m to any adjacent site.

BauO NW, § 6 (Building Code Northrhine- Westphalia)
The distances of the volume to
two adjacent sites are below the
minimum allowed.

BauGB § 9, Pt. 2 (Federal German Building Law)
Development-Plan Nr. 68419/02
dated 17.08.1970
The volume in its entirety exceeds the
maximum allowed construction on
that site.

BauGB § 9, Pt. 2 (Federal German Building Law)
Development-Plan Nr. 68419/02
dated 17.08.1970
The building exceeds the
building limit, as defined
in the development plan.

BauO NW, § 17, BauO NW, § 35
Fire-regulations: the necessary
escape staircase is not located alongside
an external wall.

DschG, § 1, Pt. 1,
(law of historical landmarks)
The gate as a historical
landmark has a nonharmonious
construction
adjacent to (over) it.

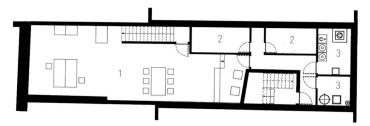

Level -1

1. Filing room (for the office)
2. Cellars
3. Machinery rooms

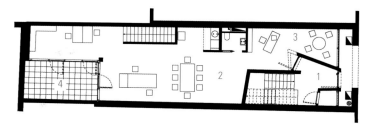

Level 0

1. Common entrance area
2. Office unit
3. Reception / waiting/talking
4. Inner court

Level 1

Lower apartment:
1. Hall, Living
2. Cooking, eating
3. Living, working
4. Terrace

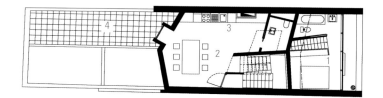

Nivel 2

Lower apartment:
1. Sleeping
Upper Apartment:
2. Entrance, eating
3. Cooking
4. Terrace

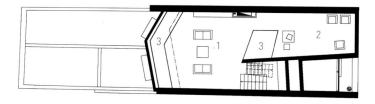

Nivel 3

Upper apartment:
1. Living, celebrating
2. Reading, watching TV
3. Attics

Nivel 4

Tal
1. Working
2. Sleeping
3. Attics

Longitudinal sections

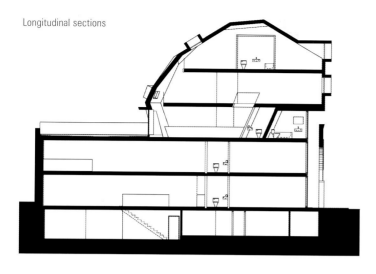

Axonometric sections

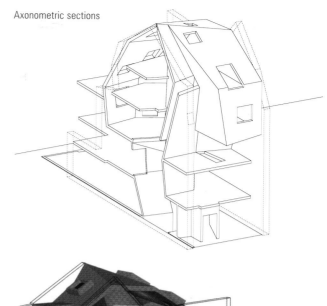

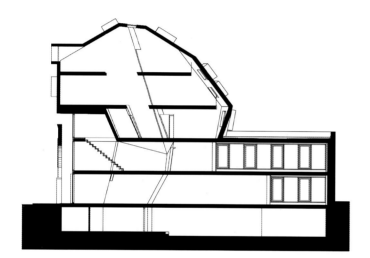

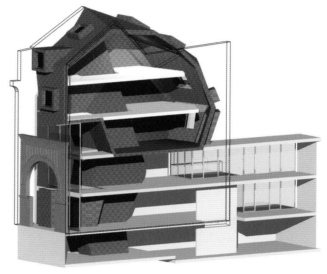

Cross sections

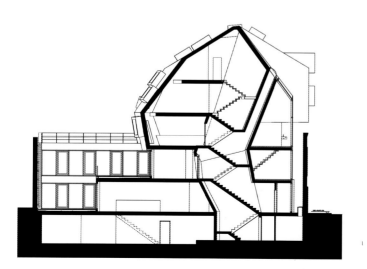

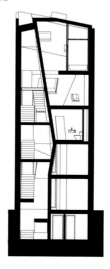

225

The interior unfolds throughout the five floors in a geometrically anarchistic progression.

The only parallel lines shaping the space are those of the structural system, while the walls, voids and railings break up the orthogonality.

227

Atelier Tekuto
Cell Brick House

Tokyo, Japan

Cell Brick House sits on the corner lot of a tranquil Tokyo residential area. Tokyo based architect Yasuhiro Yamashita constructed the building, and the skin layering helps create a unique dwelling that applies a new form of masonry. He calls this form of construction "void masonry". The boxes do not serve just to make structure, but also become storage units in the house's interior. They also work to create a brise-soleil light control, allowing the building to respond to the heat of the environment.

The steel boxes used here measure 900 x 450 x 300 mm, and the thickness of the portion facing outside stands at 9 mm. By piling them up in units rather than individually they succeeded in creating a modern design. Since the assembled box units do not fit together perfectly, light is brought into the interior at periodic intervals.

Among the several novel ideas that the client proposed for the project, one example is the bathroom, which is situated so as to appear to be floating; another such idea incorporated into the design was the washing machine sitting on the way up a spiral staircase.

The building takes up three levels from the first floor basement to the above ground second floor. The ground area encompasses 32.93 m² with a total built area of 85.05 m², and a height of 6.685 meters. In the next project, they constructed the structure of glass blocks, semi-translucent blocks and transparent blocks, instead of steel boxes.

Photographs: Makoto Yoshida

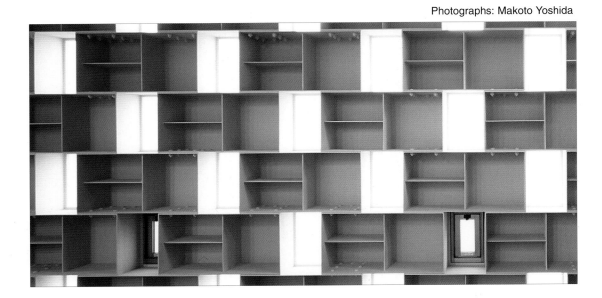

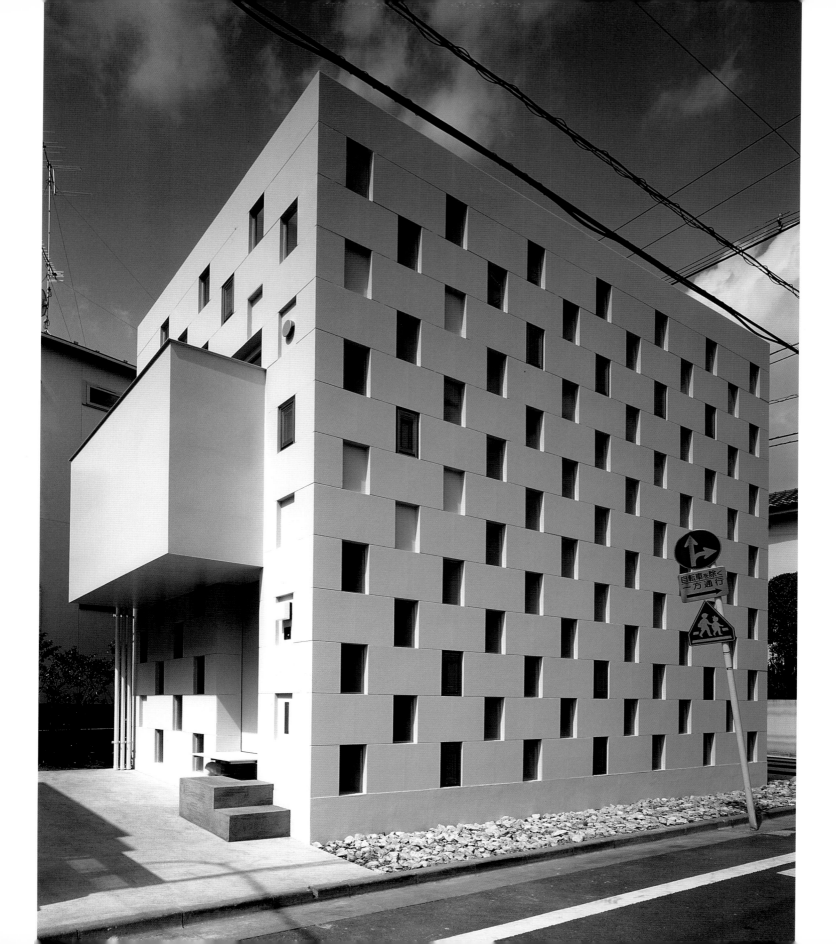

At first glance, the Cell Brick House seems to be a structure of piled-up concrete blocks, but on closer inspection one sees that these blocks are in fact steel boxes.

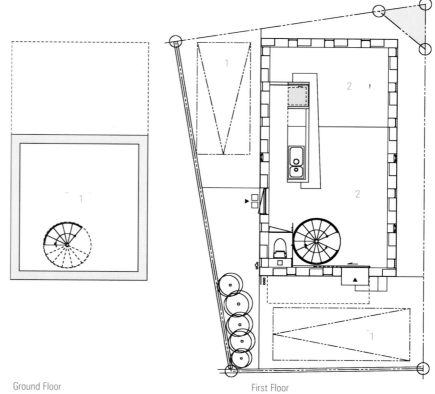

Ground Floor

1. Room 1

First Floor

1. Car
2. Dining-living room
3. Bedroom

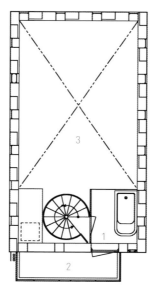

Second Floor

1. Bathroom
2. Terrace
3. Void

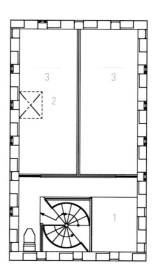

Third Floor

1. Loft
2. Top light
3. Bedroom

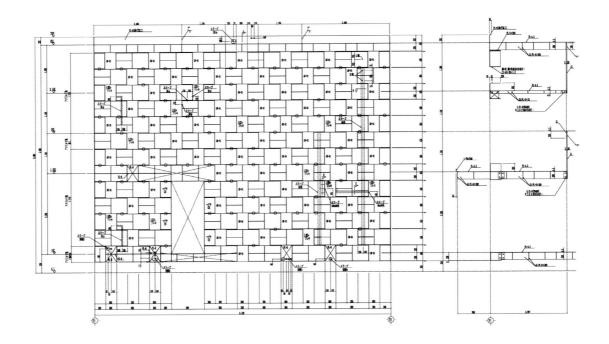

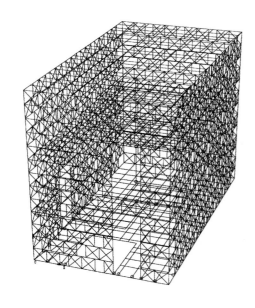

Model analysis

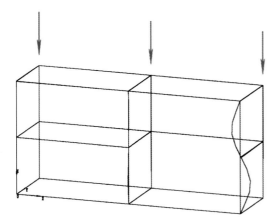

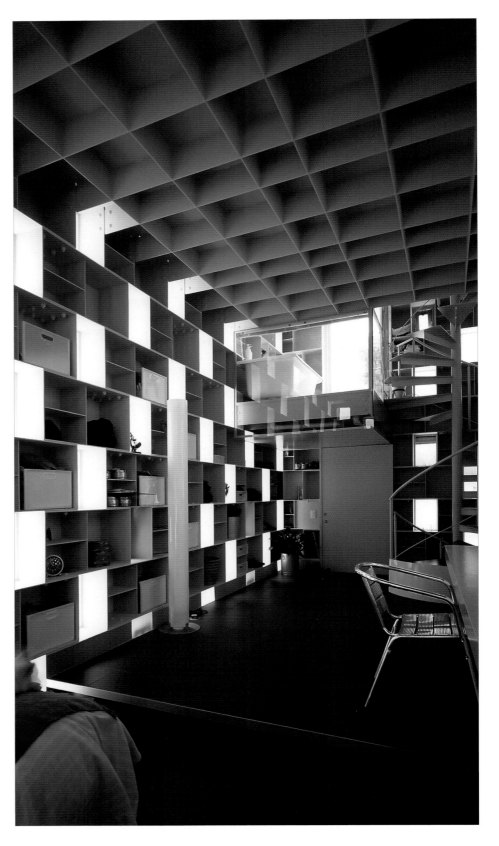

The house is for a family of three: a single parent and two children. The facade's composition of alternating steel blocks and voids is seen in the interior as a succession of storage spaces broken up by dozens of windows that bring abundant natural light into the home.